It Is Appointed Unto Men

ENDORSEMENTS

Appointed Unto Men is a fascinating account of one family's multi-generational involvement with The Salvation Army. In telling the story of the family, the history of The Salvation Army is also told, not from the prospective of the great leaders but from people who felt that the Lord had led them into the organization where they served with joy and great dedication. This foot soldiers view makes great reading by providing insights and stories that thrill, challenge and always interest.

Major Allen Satterlee
Editor-in-Chief and National Literary Secretary
The Salvation Army National Headquarters
Alexandria, Virginia

It has been fascinating to assist the Payton family in writing this biography of their grandmother Margaret Elizabeth Phillipa Bach. As I have read the chapters I have noted how they have firmly positioned Margaret's story in the context of the Victorian era and the early years of The Salvation Army. Margaret's story is one of so many unsung heroes without whose commitment and loyal service our Army would not have prospered. I am sure their family will be inspired and if possible a wider audience too.

Major Stephen Grinsted, Director
The Salvation Army International Heritage Center
London, England

The writers take us on an intriguing and inspirational journey as they trace the family history of Margaret Bach and George Payton, early Salvation Army officers. The journey which begins in the small community in Ohio continues in Reading, England and the small market town of Wokingham in south east England during the early days of The Salvation Army. It crosses the Atlantic to encompass both the United States and Canada. It is a fascinating journal of the faithfulness of God and the rigors and challenges faced by those who were willing to answer the call to Salvation Army Officership. An interesting read that reaffirms God's faithfulness.

Colonel John Carew, Director
The Salvation Army Heritage Center
Toronto, Canada

It Is Appointed Unto Men

The Payton Family

Copyright © 2013 by The Payton Family.

Library of Congress Control Number:		2013908898
ISBN:	Hardcover	978-1-4836-4173-7
	Softcover	978-1-4836-4172-0
	Ebook	978-1-4836-4174-4

All rights reserved. No part of this book may be reproduced or transmitted in any form or by any means, electronic or mechanical, including photocopying, recording, or by any information storage and retrieval system, without permission in writing from the copyright owner.

This book was printed in the United States of America.

Rev. date: 06/07/2013

To order additional copies of this book, contact:
Xlibris Corporation
1-888-795-4274
www.Xlibris.com
Orders@Xlibris.com

Contents

Dedication Page 7
The Authors 9
Acknowledgements 11
Foreword 13
Introduction 17

Peril at Sea 19
A Watershed Decade 27
A Life Changing Experience 31
The Wokingham Corps 37
Preparing For The Battle 42
On to the Conflict 52
Continuing the Conflict 57
A New Life in a New World 68
New Horizons 82
Finding Her Love 91
Reengagement in the Battle 102
Pioneering in Western Ontario 115
Who Was George Charles Payton? 138
Hamilton and Beyond 145

Epilogue 151
Appendix I: The Army A, B, Cs 155
Appendix II: Interesting Facts 157

DEDICATED TO LOUISA, EDWIN, FLOSSIE & HAROLD

(The children of George and Margaret Payton)

We are the beneficiaries of their legacy. They shared many of these stories.

Second row—Elsie Payton, Gilbert Bryant, Edwin Payton, Esther Payton, Harold Payton, Flossie Holder.
First row—Louisa Bryant, Margaret Elizabeth Phillipa Bach Payton.

THE AUTHORS

The Payton Family

In August of 2009, the members of the informal Payton Historical Society first met for the purpose of researching and recording this story. It has grown beyond what we imagined. Gradually we created a skeleton of what we wanted to say. Different portions of the book were written by various committee members. As the texts were completed, they were brought to a weekly meeting during which time suggestions and corrections were made. We are, in ascending order of age, Margaret Payton Seltrecht Crocker and Frank, Harold, George and Ernest Payton. We wish to express special appreciation to Joan Fenner Payton who spent many hours editing the manuscript. We share this story with you trusting that it will be an inspiration of how God can make people instruments to accomplish His purposes.

God leads, interrupts, and brings people and events together, for His purposes.

Acknowledgements

Five people have been intimately involved in the production of this book for almost four years. They are Ernest, George, Harold, and Frank Payton, also Margaret Payton Seltrecht Crocker. The committee usually met once a week. George was the first to make an effort to unearth some of the details of our family story as he accumulated material prior to the commencement of this endeavor. Through a year-long subscription to www.Ancestry.com, he unearthed the basic information of the family tree. He also spent time reading old issues of the *Canadian War Cry* and other material in addition to writing portions of the manuscript. Ernest has contributed an appreciable amount of material from his files and his memory, plus doing some of the writing. Frank has spent many hours reading and copying articles from past issues of the *London War Cry*, the *American War Cry*, the *Canadian War Cry* as well as the *New York Times*. He also has written part of the manuscript. Harold and Margaret have unearthed additional material which has enhanced the entire story. In addition, the five of us wish to express our appreciation to the following persons or entities:

1. General Paul Radar for writing the forward.
2. Mr. Charles Olsen and Mr. Robert McLees of the USA Eastern Territorial Headquarters Document Management Bureau which facilitated the availability of the *London War Cry* and *New York War Cry* microfilm.
3. Mrs. Susan Mitchem and the staff of The Salvation Army National Headquarters Archive & Research Department for providing material at our request.
4. Major Allen Satterlee, National Literary Secretary for his support of the book.

5. Major Stephen Grinsted and the staff of the International Heritage Center in London, England.
6. Colonel John Carew and the staff of the Heritage Center of the Canadian Territory.
7. Joan Fenner Payton for editing the manuscript.
8. Bernard Smith, historian of the Reading, England, Corps.
9. The Tompkins County Public Library for the use of their microfilm facilities and the availability of the microfilm library of the New York Times from the 1850s.
10. The John E. T. Milsaps Collection, Houston Metropolitan Research Center, Houston, Texas, Public Library for the availability of early Salvation Army publications and the provision of digital copies of photographs which are unavailable elsewhere.
11. The Dorian, Ontario, municipality for historical material.
12. The Peterborough Examiner, Peterborough, Ontario, Canada.
13. Several members of the family (cousins) for providing photographs and shared stories they remember from their parents.
14. To Joy Payton Roe for the cover design and art work and Mark Payton for his contributed art work.
15. Our wives for assisting with the grammar.

Foreword

The Salvation Army in North America—and indeed, around the world, is gifted with the respect, confidence and generous support of the public. These blessings were not free. They were purchased with blood, sweat and tears. We owe these priceless, though fragile, assets to the dauntless courage and bold faith of generations of heroic Salvationists who have gone before us. The saga of their love and loyalty to God and the Army illumines the pages of the great Salvation story.

These were women and men with a passionate allegiance to the Army's mission. They were women and men fearless in the face of opposition, misunderstanding and physical attack. To read their story is to tread on holy ground. Like the early apostles, they were often "hard pressed on every side, but not crushed; perplexed but not in despair; persecuted, but not abandoned; struck down, but not destroyed" (2 Cor. 4:8-9). Margaret (Maggie) Bach, a progenitor of the Army's Payton legacy, was just such an 'undauntable.' Born in Ohio in 1862, her family returned to their native England when she was five. There she met the Army in 1881, just three years after the movement had taken the name: The Salvation Army. By September of 1882 she was a Cadet preparing to be a Salvation Army officer at the Clapton Training Home in London. Within months she was thrust into the thick of the battle for souls. And a battle it surely was. Maggie demonstrated a holy 'chuztpa' in confronting the opposition to her ministry. The Army was advancing at a torrid pace. The battle was hot and costly. It took its toll. The dangers were real and the casualties many. No place for the faint of spirit. These early warriors were in the grip of a compelling passion for the lost. No price was too great. No danger too daunting. They would follow the Blood and Fire banner wherever it might take them in glad obedience to their Heavenly Captain.

Having relocated to Canada in 1889 Margaret met and married a Salvationist bandsman and blacksmith, George Charles Payton, and thus began a marvelous family tradition that continues on in devotion to God and the Army to this day. The way was not easy. Taxed to the limit by the intense demands of the salvation war, Margaret required a number of short breaks to recoup her strength. Eventually a breakdown in health made necessary an extended sick furlough. Her husband who had joined her as an officer in 1895 was required to relinquish active service just five years later for health reasons. Their final appointment was in Buffalo, New York. The family moved to a small rural community in western Ontario, Canada where George returned for a time to his trade as a blacksmith in order to support his family. He was promoted to Glory in 1917. The family continued on in their loyalty to the Army, Margaret serving as a faithful soldier until her 'promotion to Glory' in 1945.

It is a gripping story and reveals much regarding the challenges and triumphs of those early formative days of Army mission, in England, Canada and the United States. Among other distinctive aspects of the Army mission, it illustrates and validates the commitment of William and Catherine Booth, co-founders of The Salvation Army, to equal opportunity for women in ministry and leadership. Indeed, William Booth averred: "Some of my best men are women!" Valiant women of Maggie Bach's company, anointed and gifted by the Spirit to preach and lead, were in the vanguard of the Army's remarkable advance from the very earliest days and have been ever since. God has honored their service and leadership with 'souls for their hire' despite the insistence of well-meaning nay-sayers that God does not intend for women to preach or lead. Our founders were not about to disqualify half their fighting force and more. Nor could they afford to with a world to be won.

Further, the Payton story highlights the critical role of faithful soldiers and local officers who maintain our witness in local corps and communities all across the Army world.

God loves nothing more than to work savingly across the generations, causing the vision to be passed from generation to generation. His promises of blessing are pledged "to a thousand generations" of those who love him and keep his commandments (Deuteronomy 5:10). The salvation story unfolds in Scripture across the generations. There is a truth in the saying that 'God has no grandchildren.' "In Christ Jesus you are all children of God by faith" (Galatians 3:26). But thank God, some of us are blessed with a heritage of faith. We have grandparents and parents, and great grandparents, who have lived the faith they taught and have been used of the Spirit to engender in our hearts a passion and purpose to follow them as they have followed Christ (1 Cor. 11:1). That is the story of the Payton family, from the Army's earliest battles until this day and beyond. And there is so much more to the story yet to be lived and written to the glory of God.

This is one family's saga of faith and obedience in the ranks of The Salvation Army, carefully researched and engagingly recorded in these pages by the four Payton siblings: Ernest, George, Frank and Margaret and cousin Harold. It will be for all of us a stimulus to fresh commitment, sustained devotion, and a Spirit-inspired determination to cherish the flame and pass the 'fire' to the next generation.

General Paul A. Rader (Ret.)
Lexington, Kentucky
April 2013

Artist Mark Payton

Introduction

Margaret Elizabeth Phillipa Bach (Payton)

"If thou faint in the day of adversity, thy strength is small."
Proverbs 24:10 KJV

One Sunday afternoon, Captain Margaret Bach received a note from the Society of Infidels threatening to refute the veracity of anything that she would read from the Bible that night in the Huddersfield Corps (church) in Yorkshire, England.[1] She had been a Salvation Army officer for some two years and knew the rigors of being a pioneer in the early days of the Army. The year was 1884. She had already experienced opposition to the cause and ministry of the organization, but this was entirely unexpected. What portion of Scripture should she read? What should she preach about? Since she had only a grade school education and just fourteen weeks of formal training for the ministry, she was understandably nervous. The Salvation Army was growing rapidly during those days of persecution. Its motivation was misunderstood as well as the meaning of its ministry. An atheist group was bent on disrupting the Army's worship services both on the street and in their worship center. The Sunday night meetings were held in the Armory, the largest gathering place in the city, just across the street from the atheist society's headquarters.

---

[1] Canadian *War Cry*. Jan. 5, 1929. p. 6.

Margaret prayed and poured over her Bible and pondered in her mind to find some way to meet the challenge. She turned the early leadership of the meeting to her lieutenant to have time to collect her thoughts. No inspiration came even as the meeting progressed. About ten minutes before she was to speak, the Lord clearly inspired her to read Hebrews 9:27, "And as it is appointed unto men once to die . . . ." (King James Version) After reading this, she closed the Bible and looked to the leader of the atheists as he stood with his Bible open to the passage. He returned the look—there was silence in the room. His followers, who filled one entire section of the hall, waited eagerly for him to respond. He was waiting for Margaret to continue and read the phrase, " . . . after that the judgment." But she never did.

After several moments of silence, Margaret began to preach on the certainty that all must die and that only the Bible offers any assurance of hope beyond the grave. The leader remained standing for about five minutes, and then he sat down. When the invitation for decisions was made, the entire group of atheists left. Never again did they trouble the Salvationists.

This was just one of the many challenging experiences that Margaret, often referred to as Maggie Bach in Army publications, would encounter during her early days of Salvation Army officership in England, her transfer to Canada, her marriage to George Payton and their Christian service together. We will endeavor to share these stories with you, but first we need to give you some background of what brought her to this defiant confrontation.

Chapter One

Peril at Sea

"These see the works of the Lord, and his wonders in the deep."
Psalm 107:24 KJV

In the winter of 1857, James Bach was desperately worried as he walked the streets of New York City. The ship his wife was sailing on was over a month late and having heard nothing, he was beginning to fear the worst. He found no comfort as he read the *New York Times*; the newspaper was filled with catastrophes at sea. He may have read about the ship New York encountering a constant succession of gales for eighty days of her passage. In twenty five years at sea, the Captain had never experienced so much rough weather.[2] Also reading of the fate of the ship Confederation being "blown ashore on the New Jersey coast and becoming a total wreck," would only deepen his concern.[3] Two days later the *Times* carried the story of the bark (vessel) Hershel "with 188 German immigrants aboard arriving wholly out of provisions and water. In this condition she was locked in ice . . . they were in imminent peril of starvation."[4]

On one of his walks, James came upon a storefront church. Having nothing better to do, he walked in as the service was in progress. This may have been an opportunity to take his mind off the tragic news he expected

---

[2] *New York Times.* Dec. 24, 1856.
[3] *New York Times.* Feb. 7, 1857.
[4] *New York Times.* Feb. 9, 1857.

to hear at any moment. Sometime during the service, he began to listen to the message of the evangelist. It was bringing comfort to his troubled spirit. During the call for commitment, "The woman evangelist came down to deal with him to find what his troubles were. He told her and she led him to the Lord." The first name of the evangelist was Margaret. James thought, "If our family is reunited and my wife gives birth to a daughter I will name her Margaret." The evangelist made an impact on the family that reaches down through many generations.[5]

While reviewing the 1857 issues of the *New York Times,* the name of a particular woman evangelist was noted on many occasions. Women evangelists were rare in the 1850s, and Margaret L. Bishop was one of those exceptions. Her husband, John Bishop, was the leader, and Margaret was the preacher of the Christian Israelite Church whose mission was located at 108 First Street near the Hudson River piers in New York City. It is most likely that Margaret L. Bishop was the one who led James Bach to the Lord at that mission.[6]

It is possible that James was second-guessing himself. He may have been thinking, "Why had we not traveled together? Why did I leave my native England and family?" Two years after the death of his first wife of forty years, Mary Sutton Grooms, James married Louisa Hic Worley from Reading, England. A child was born to them, but in a month and a half, their joy was turned to sorrow when Mary Martha died. James' family strongly opposed the marriage because of the disparity in their ages—he being sixty and Louisa only nineteen. In their mind it was scandalous, and his nine older siblings practically disowned him. With heartbreak and family estrangement, a fresh start in the New World seemed to be the answer.

Grandson Edwin relayed the story shared through the generations that James could not know that far out in the Atlantic Ocean, the ship Louisa was sailing on was in serious trouble. They encountered a fierce storm that broke off the rudder. (The report of the ship "Middlesex Parelee" that lost its rudder could fit into the time frame of Louisa's trip.)[7] Without the ability to control their course, they floundered about the ocean until a miracle took place. The crew of another ship on the way to New York sighted them and sensed their

---

[5] Payton, Edwin V. (Grandson of James Bach), Personal interview. 1983.
[6] *New York Times.* Mar. 14, 1857.
[7] *New York Times.* Apr. 16, 1857.

distress. Fortunately they were able to tow the crippled ship to shore. What a joyful, however belated, reunion took place on a New York pier.

The family settled down to life in the city. James, a thirty-third degree Mason made enough contacts to find work and support his family. On December 10, 1857, their first son was born. He was given the name of his father and a second name which reflected the name of the city of his father's birthplace, thus, James Aston. He was baptized at All Saints Church on January 17, 1858. A second boy was born August 12, 1860. The first name, Richard, honored his grandfather and his second name, William, was a name found in all but one generation back to 1641. William, as he was called, was baptized at All Saints Church on October 14, 1860. Little is known of their life in New York City.

James' brother William, eight years his senior, had emigrated from England to Coshocton County, Ohio, with his wife Mary and their five children in the 1840s. It would appear that years had brought healing in the family, and James thought it was time to reconnect so he made the decision to move his family to Ohio. We do not know the mode of transportation the family used. The Pennsylvania Railroad and the Baltimore and Ohio had service to the Ohio River. The New York Central connected New York City to Buffalo. Another possible means of transportation was the Erie Canal and the Ohio & Erie Canal.

On August 21, 1830, the first canal boat to stop in Roscoe, Ohio, just outside of Coshocton, was the Monticello. By whatever means, sometime during the early years of the American Civil War, the family arrived in the bustling canal town of Roscoe. We have no information about the family reunion that took place when James and William met in Coshocton County. We can only assume that it was a joyful occasion.

The James Bach family lived in several of the communities in the county. We suppose that their first home was in Roscoe. This is based on the fact that on July 29, 1862, James and William welcomed a sister to their home, Margaret Elizabeth Phillipa Bach. Her first name honored the woman evangelist who led James to the Lord. Her second name honored Elizabeth, the mother of James. She was baptized at the E. P. Methodist Church on August 21, 1862, in Roscoe, Ohio. At that same time the town was buzzing about one of the two town fathers, Noah Swayne. President Lincoln appointed him Associate Justice of the Supreme Court in 1862.

The Ohio and Erie Canal
Artist Mark Payton

The Village of Roscoe Ohio.
Artist, Mark Payton.

Roscoe was a thriving community at that time. The town could boast of harness, blacksmith and cooper's shops, foundry, brickyard, pottery, mills and much more. The Ohio and Erie Canal was responsible for the years of growth since the opening in 1830, but the times were about to change. The people could already see the handwriting on the wall. The railroads had begun to move into Ohio in the 1850s and across the river into Coshocton in the 1860s. This may be one of the reasons the Bach family moved to the eastern part of Coshocton County and Oxford Township. The fact that James' brother William lived in Oxford Township would have been a further attraction. Family oral history indicates that James was a teacher in a West Lafayette school. It is believed that the family lived in several different residences in Oxford Township. We know of one, the Old Stone Fort, located south of the Tuscarawas River. In later years Margaret repeatedly referred to the small fort building with wedge windows to facilitate shooting at the Indians from a wide angle. It is within sight of the cemetery where her father James Bach would later be buried. Her brother James Aston Bach was buried in a cemetery across the river. When her son Edwin saw the fort many years later, he said it was exactly like the one his mother described.

The Old Stone Fort.

Interior of the Old Stone Fort, left to right, (son)
Edwin and his wife Elsie Payton.

One of the mysteries of Ohio history is the identity of the builder of this Fort. Most historians agree that the Stone Fort is the oldest existing building west of the Appalachian Mountains. The National Society Colonial Dames XVII plaque reads, "Believed to have been built by De´Iberville, LaSallés successor, who built French Forts in the Mississippi valley [from] 1679 to 1689. He located one northeast of the Ohio River. This may be that fort and Ohio's oldest building." The family is convinced that this was the residence of the James Bach family and possibly their last Ohio home since the two cemeteries are nearby where other members of the Bach family are buried. How a family of five could have managed in a fourteen foot square space and a loft is a question that has never been answered.

The family endured a tragedy when Margaret was only one year and four months old. Her oldest brother James Ashton Bach died December 2, 1863. He was buried in the Evansburgh Cemetery across the Tuscarawas River from the Old Stone Fort. Life on the Ohio frontier was difficult and providing for his family was a daily challenge. At the age of seventy-two and after a lingering illness, James Bach died on November 26, 1867.[8] The family lived on the edge of poverty and was unable to provide a suitable funeral. Since Mr. Bach was a thirty-third degree Mason, the organization paid thirty dollars for his coffin and ten dollars for a burial suit. It is believed that his large gravestone in the Oxford Township Cemetery was purchased by the Roscoe Masonic Lodge. With no means of support, Louisa decided that it would be prudent to return to her family in Reading, England. It is also believed that support for the transportation came from the Masonic Lodge. After a near catastrophic trip to America, Louisa must have viewed her return trip with seven-year old William and five-year old Margaret with much apprehension.

James Bach's tombstone—Oxford Township, Coshocton, County.

Margaret would have few memories of life in Ohio. Two of them that she talked about were watching the soldiers returning from the Civil War and living in the Old Stone Fort. The fact that she was born in the United States would have a profound effect on her life in future years.

---

[8] Klossen, John. Letter. Minutes of the Roscoe, Ohio, Lodge, No. 190 F & A.M. Apr. 2, 1900.

Nothing is known of the family until their names appeared in the 1871 English Census "... Louisa Hic Bach, thirty-five, lived in Haffordshire, West Bromwich, with Margaret Elizabeth (eight) and Richard William (ten)." In the intervening years, she met the widower Robert C. Goodchild who was raising his three boys, Charles, William and Robert. They were married in early 1872. Ten more silent years passed before the 1881 English Census locates them in her home town of Reading, England.

Chapter Two

A Watershed Decade

"One generation shall praise thy works to another, and shall declare thy mighty acts."

Psalm 145:4 KJV

Whereas there is little known of Margaret Bach's growing-up years, it is a fact that in Victorian England there were great divides among the rich, the middle class and the poor. These groups lived in extremely different worlds, and there was little communication between them. It was during this time that the Industrial Revolution took place. This caused a great migration from rural areas to the larger cities with the hope of finding employment. However, along with this came overpopulation, which resulted in crowded and unhealthy living conditions amply described by Charles Dickens in his various novels. It also was the breeding ground for a myriad of vices that complicated the problem. The rich turned to activities such as the arts which included music, fox hunting and horse racing for entertainment. But the poor gravitated to gambling, drinking and prostitution. Into this needy Victorian world, God called The Salvation Army into being through the inspired ministry of William and Catherine Booth.

The East London Revival Society was born in 1865 which later became the East London Christian Mission and then again changed its name to The Christian Mission as it reached other parts of the country. Two years before the beginning of the decade of the 1880s, the final name change took place, and it became The Salvation Army. With the change in name, this evangelistic organization took on a new impetus, and it began to spread rapidly all across the country. This truly was a watershed decade because of its expansion. Not only did it grow in the British Isles, but it began its outreach to other countries. It might be said that this decade was the fastest growing decade in all the history of the Army.[9] In 1878 there were 36 corps (churches), and in 1888 there were 2,413. In 1878 there were 195 officers, and in 1888 there were 6,391. During this decade, the Army spread to a total of 19 countries.[10]

It was a decade of initiatives:

- The first formal training of candidates for officership was established.
- Whereas there had been some effort to meet the physical needs of people, a formal social work program was started during this time. These statistics will readily illustrate the growth of this program. In 1880 there was one rescue home in the east end of London,[11] and by 1890 there were 89 different expressions of social work. Another initiative that started during this time was the "Cellar, Gutter and Garret Brigade" which visited the extremely poor, the elderly and the ill. The purpose was to help them clean their homes and to care for those in need therein. This program continued for many years.[12]
- The first doctrine book was published in 1881.
- The ministry of women grew exponentially
- This period saw the beginning of the brass bands as part of Army ministry.

It was during this time that the younger children of the Founders began to take responsibilities in leadership. The Army also started to have huge united gatherings—the largest being the very first International Congress in 1886.[13] This was so large that they were not able to meet in one building but had simultaneous events in several large meeting halls. One of the most noteworthy undertakings during this period, with the help of a large daily publication, was the campaign to have the Parliament change the age of

---

[9] Sandall, Robert. *History of The Salvation Army*, Vol. II. London: The Salvation Army, 1950. Chapt. 1.
[10] Sandall, Vol. II, p. 338.
[11] Sandall. Vol. II, p. 66.
[12] Sandall. Vol. III, p. 74.
[13] Sandall. Vol. III, p. 298.

consent from fourteen to eighteen. After a thorough investigation of the prostitution trade, W. T. Stead, editor of the Pall Mall Gazette, with the help of The Salvation Army, wrote a series of articles in his publication entitled "The Maiden Tribute of Modern Babylon." This created an uproar in the population, and in the end, the age of consent was changed from fourteen to sixteen. In the process, the editor, Bramwell Booth (son of the Founder) and one other were taken to court resulting in the editor and the other person going to prison for several months.[14]

This decade is also remembered for the period when great steps of faith were made in the acquisitions of large auditoriums. The Founder acquired what had been an orphanage and renovated it to create Clapton Congress Hall which could hold thousands. The Eagle which had been a bar and The Grecian theater which was able to seat thousands was also purchased. At the same time, organized opposition against the Army under the name of the Skeleton Army arose with its black flag bearing a skull and cross bones as their symbol. This was a period of opposition not only on the part of the liquor interests but also of some church leaders. There was an effort on the part of some of the Church of England leaders to co-opt this growing movement and make it part of the established church. The effort failed.

As the decade was coming to a close, William Booth was diligently writing, with the help of two officers, his landmark book, *In Darkest England and the Way Out*, which was to revolutionize social work in Great Britain.[15]

The decade concluded with the severe illness of the co-founder, Catherine Booth. Catherine's death in 1890, was a huge loss, not only to William and the family but to the Army as well. Much of what the Army eventually became was a result of the various difficulties and decisions made during this tumultuous decade.

In his book, *Heathen England*, Commissioner George Scott Railton in 1879 observed in detail the reasons why the Army grew as fast as it did.

Why we succeed:

1. The Army succeeds by aiming at immediate results.
2. The Army succeeds by making the most of the converts.

---

[14] Sandall. Vol. III, p. 31.
[15] Sandall. Vol. III. p. 62.

3. The Army succeeds by teaching converts to be holy.
4. The Army succeeds by teaching its hearers to do their utmost towards meeting the expenses of the work.[16]

We would like to add, in our opinion, that God saw there were many people who were in need of moral and spiritual redemption and raised up The Salvation Army to be a militant group to fill that need.

In 1881 Margaret Elizabeth Phillipa Bach met this Army for the first time, and it was to mold her life and set her on a path that was to influence not only many during her lifetime but continues to do so through her descendents.

---

[16] Railton. George Scott. *Heathen England*. London: S. W. Partridge & Co., 1879. p. 134.

Chapter Three

A Life Changing Experience

"Let no man despise thy youth; but be thou an example of the believers, in word, in conversation, in charity, in spirit, in faith, in purity."
I Timothy 4:12 KJV

At the age of twenty-one, Richard William Bach had been living away from home for some time. When he returned, he was wearing a Salvation Army uniform which concerned his mother. She asked her nineteen-year old daughter, Margaret, to go with him to investigate this new and unfamiliar organization. The nearest town was Reading where they were "opening fire" on Wednesday, March 30, 1881. It is possible that Richard William had returned home because he knew that the Army was about to establish its newest operation near his home.

READING BOATHOUSE CORPS

"Opening Fire" was the term that was used in those days, and it was an apt description of what happened. The abandoned building they used was called The Boathouse as it was situated by the River Kennet. It had a large meeting room with a dirt floor and could be compared to the revival tent meetings of more recent times. Crowds were being attracted to this novel religious group that used unorthodox methods to attract and capture new converts. There is no better way to describe what was happening than to quote portions of a few articles that appeared in the *War Cry* (a twice-weekly publication). It will help us grasp the red hot, single purpose evangelistic fervor of the Salvationists then and the reason for their rapid progress. (Notice the common language and punctuation of the day.)

> To recognize the victories that God has got to His name in one week is an utter impossibility. I can only say that about 250 souls have wept and agonized on account of their sins and now testify to what God has wrought in giving them new hearts, new lives; in giving them new power over drink, sin, and the Devil.... I believe that most of those who led on the terrible affair of the previous Sunday, are now marching to Zion. Three of them last night asked me, with tears in their eyes, to forgive them for smashing the forms and abusing us. Thank God, we forgive as we go on.... I told him that I loved him more than any other man in Reading. He burst into tears and wept in agony.... The circus attenders say our meetings they like better than going there. Come and go to the Boat House, they will want to convert you in five minutes, if you go.[17]

It is most probable that Margaret was one of those 250 converts as she recorded that she accepted the Lord in the Reading Boathouse Corps. Further reports illustrate the impact The Salvation Army had on the community.[18]

> At the close of the short sitting of the Borough Bench on Saturday morning, the Mayor expressed the gratification of the magistrates at the fact that for the period of eight days they had had no prisoners before the Bench. Such a thing, he believed had not occurred for many years.... The Mayor made these remarks and the police inform us that not only is there a diminution in the number of prisoners, but also the streets are much quieter, and that fewer drunken persons are to be found than was the case some weeks ago. It is also a known fact that many prominent "roughs" old acquaintances of the police and the Bench, have joined The Salvation Army.[19]
>
> A publican [tavern owner] said to one of our Soldiers, 'I never see you now.' 'No, nor you never will. I'm converted, and I've joined the Army.... In the public houses [taverns] custom[ers] has fallen off

---

[17] London *War Cry.* Apr. 14, 1881.
[18] Canadian *War Cry.* Jan. 5, 1929. p. 6.
[19] *Reading Express.* Apr. 21, 1881.

to a fearful extent . . . . The churches and chapels are all awaking from their sleep, and some are going in already for Salvation to the amount of nine souls at one chapel on one Sunday night.[20]

The growth of the Reading Boathouse Corps was so great that the Founder, General William Booth, made a visit on the weekend of May 28 and 29 to share in their victories. But all was not stress free. The Salvation Army had signed a lease for The Boathouse for three years. With pressure from the breweries, the landlord decided to force them out in three months. General Booth came to deal with this situation. First, let us review some of the positive things that happened during that weekend as reported in the *War Cry*. This probably was the first of many occasions for Margaret to see The Founder.[21]

THE GENERAL AT READING

At three o'clock when our train arrived, it was evident that there was a very special state of things just outside the station, and a very large amount of expectation inside it. The attempt to form a procession proved, at first, rather difficult owing to the dense throng which filled up all the available space, and to the presence of a good many of the class whose greatest enjoyment comes from rough horse-play. With the assistance, however, of the policemen who were present, we moved off at last and after a somewhat struggling advance of fifty yards or so the crowd seemed to resolve itself into four processions, our own being the central one . . . . There had been no announcement of a meeting indoors, yet The Boathouse filled up in a very few minutes and prayer, song, and testimony were gone into with all the spirit that could be desired. Toward the close of this meeting, a fine big fellow pushed his way up to the front and insisted upon standing just before the platform. 'I want to see their faces,' he said, 'for they look good.' And although he was, to some extent, under the influence of drink, he was far from being unable to recognize or appreciate goodness and truth, in fact, he was very soon down on his knees weeping before the Lord, and acknowledging that the poor drunkard of to-day had been a preacher of years gone by . . . . The General gave one of his rousing and yet soul-stirring [messages] on The Army's birth and growth, and [assured] God's people of Reading that if we had to

---

[20] London *War Cry*. May 5, 1881.
[21] 130th Anniversary Program. Reading, England, Corps. 2011.

be [deprived] of the Boat House we would, by God's [hand] build something twice the size, and if we had to lose that we would have something larger still.[22]

Lieut. Moore writes for Capt. Skidmore:

> Thank God the past week has been a time of victory. Coming down out of the main street with our band we passed a German band, who were trying to cheer up a publican who it is said has lost nearly five pounds a week since The Army came here, but our soldiers who have got good lungs, sang in better tune than the Germans played. The publican got rather perplexed and thought to have a spree, by getting two of the Germans beside him in a trap, and driving in front of our ranks. The Captain clapped the Soldiers on the back for their pluck. Souls are shipping for glory in the "Salvation" Boathouse. Holiness meeting, on Friday, grand; many seeking the blessing of entire sanctification. Sunday a day of victory, 140 at Knee-drill; [early morning prayer meeting] time of refreshing all day; souls every meeting. Glory to God![23]
>
> Sunday was a good day to our souls. 167 at seven o'clock Knee-Drill, precious time. Good meetings all day; Salvation Boat House full, souls every meeting. Finished up the day with twenty souls, making thirty-nine for the week.[24]

Unfortunately, the time came when they had to abandon The Boathouse building, and for a time, they held their services outdoors.

> (Capt. Skidmore) Victory! Victory is now our cry, through the precious blood of the Lamb. Having no Hall, week days and Sundays we are in the open-air. Eighty at seven o'clock open-air Knee-drill glorious time.[25]
>
> This past week has been one of blessings to our souls. Mrs. Booth was with us last Thursday; real heart-searching time . . . . Saturday, Free-and-Easy [meeting]; melting testimonies. Showers of rain,

---

[22] London *War Cry.* June 9, 1881.
[23] London *War Cry.* June 16, 1881.
[24] London *War Cry.* June 30, 1881.
[25] London *War Cry.* July 21, 1881.

> showers of blessing . . . . (Sunday) Hundreds flocked to our eleven o'clock Camp Meeting, our band doing us good service. Got in good swing after a good march, when a shower of rain scattered the congregation, soldiers sticking well to their posts.[26]
>
> Although we are out in the open-air, Glory to God, He is with us . . . . Grand marches, folks looking from their windows with amazement at our Soldiers speaking of the wonders the Lord has done for them, while the rain was pouring on us.[27]

In September they rented another facility, a skating rink and continued their ministry. They had to suspend the street meetings because they attracted so many people that the building could not accommodate them.

Lieutenant Dick Moore reported in the *War Cry*:

GRAND TIMES IN THE SALVATION SKATING RINK

Lieutenant Dick Moore writes: There have been great showers of God's blessings in this town. Many homes that were once little hells upon earth are changed now to Hallelujah homes, the men getting good new suits and the women tidy bonnets, as well as Hallelujah hearts. Amongst the many converted drunkards, swearers, smokers, etc, is a man who, a short time ago, was standing outside a pub, belonging to DEATH AND COMPANY offering us a mug of beer, as we passed by, but Hallelujah, today he is soundly saved from drink, tobacco, and a drunkard's hell; also his wife is going with him to Heaven rejoicing . . . . The Salvation Skating Rink was crowded all day: night best of all.[28]

> . . . When the Army came to Reading, a publican's pet [a favorite customer]; Jack the Coalman, said he would give ten shillings, and drink another five shillings, if he could see our Boat House burnt down, but, Hallelujah, today he is gloriously saved, testifying that where he had a little hell, he has now a happy household, and a Hallelujah wife, a Hallelujah baby, a Hallelujah heart and a new suit of clothes.[29]

---

[26] London *War Cry*. Aug. 4, 1881.
[27] London *War Cry*. Aug. 18, 1881.
[28] London War Cry. Sept. 22, 1881.
[29] London *War Cry*. Sept. 29, 1881.

In spite of adversity, the ministry continued and souls continued to be saved. The good news is that in December, William Booth returned to dedicate the new building which some reports indicated had the capacity for two thousand people.[30]

A rendering of the new building that William Booth dedicated.
Artist, Mark Payton

---

[30] Smith, Bernard, Corps historian of the Reading Central Corps. Letter to Frank Payton. Dec. 3, 2009.

Chapter Four

The Wokingham Corps

"I know thy works: behold, I have set before thee an open door, and no man can shut it: for thou hast a little strength, and hast kept my word, and hast not denied my name."

Revelation 3:8 KJV

At the same time as the dedication of the Reading building, according to official Salvation Army records, a new corps was opened just seven miles from there. The extent of the explosive growth of the corps, obviously, was not limited to the city. Transportation in the 1880s was not as we know it today, and since the Salvationists would not use public transportation on Sunday, they walked. For this reason it was necessary to open new branches in nearby towns. Is it possible that the opening of the work in Wokingham was partly because the Bach/Goodchild family and others were there ready to be part of this new outreach? We will never know, but it is conceivable. No longer would the seven mile Sunday morning trek to Knee Drill be necessary. On December 18, 1881, in the town of Wokingham with a population of 3,100 people, a corps was officially opened under the leadership of Captain W. Lucas. As happened in Reading and in most of the places where the Army "opened fire," there was opposition, but also there were positive results as well from their attacks on the evils caused by sin. In a couple of the *War Cry* articles of the time, there were hints that this was true. Several articles illustrate this:

> WOKINGHAM (Captain W. Lucas) On Tuesday, Capt. George, the converted drunkard, was with us when we went to the open-air.

A great mob was waiting for us. As soon as we struck up to sing, the people began to yell, and the devil began to growl, and his soldiers began to stone us. One stone struck the Captain on the eye, but it did not stop us; we went on, singing, to the Barracks. When we began the meeting inside, another stone came through the window. The glass flew all over the soldiers. Then we had a good meeting, one soul at the close. Bless the Lord! Sunday was a high day. "Hallelujah Fanny," with her tambourine [was] followed by a great crowd of people—just the sort we came after. The police are very kind to us. They have orders to be at every meeting. God bless them. Barracks full, afternoon and night. The night meeting was a melting time, and at the close seven prisoners captured for the Master.[31]

Praise God! We are still going into it here. A Sergeant of the Police says that he will stand by us as long as he has got a leg to stand upon, because of the good work we are doing, he has less work to do. The 'Happy Fiddler' said before he was converted, he was a respectable blackguard, but now he is saved, and can walk five miles to, and five miles from the meeting. One brother has been turned out of doors [from his home] for belonging to the Army. But he still means to fight on. Praise the Lord![32]

. . . There are twelve or thirteen public houses to let, in a little town like Wokingham. One recently opened is now shut up. The landlord of another [public] house went out four miles to seek work, and said that The Salvation Army had come to Wokingham and took his custom[ers] away, so that he had to go to work now.

Private Dot writes: "The Salvation Army is doing some good here. Some of the worst characters have been picked up out of the gutter of sin, and have found peace in the crucified Saviour. Although there has been much opposition, yet God works in a marvelous way . . . ."[33]

Officers' appointments were for short periods of time. It was normal that officers would move every three to six months, and this is demonstrated by an

---

[31] London *War Cry.* Jan. 19, 1882.
[32] London *War Cry.* Mar. 9, 1882.
[33] London *War Cry.* Apr. 6, 1882.

article published in the April 20, 1882, *War Cry*, "(Captain William Lucas.) On Sunday last our Captain and his Hallelujah wife bade farewell [after only four months]. They told us to be faithful and strong in the Lord and to go on and push the battle to the end."

Based on the few times that we saw Grandmother, we have always pictured her as a quiet reserved person, but as we read these accounts we have to remember that she was about nineteen years old and audacious in her newly found faith. We'd like to think that she was just as enthusiastic as the rest which was reported in the following:

> On Monday, being Whitsuntide, [Christian Festival of Pentecost] we had our first Salvation Fete [religious celebration] and tea, to which upwards of 100 sat down. Afterwards we had a good hour's march, firing away, with seventy in our ranks, and our band of ten in number and four sisters with tambourines at the front. [Was Margaret one of the four?] We had an A-one meeting inside, which a friend of the Army belonging to another branch of God's work led.[34]

We learn of another officer farewelling from the Corps by July 13, but the march goes on.

> Sergeant H. Corbishley writes:—Sunday was a grand time; good open-air musters. Barracks packed at night; forty spoke of the saving power of God. We wound up with a hallelujah ´finish´ and two souls in the fountain that washes whiter than snow. To God be the glory! (Captain Nellie Thorn)[35]

Before leaving the Wokingham story, we need to share two events that took place following Richard and Margaret's departure in September 1882 for the Training Home in Clapton Congress Hall. Apparently the support of the police that was enjoyed in the first months in Wokingham had changed as the following two reports indicate. In the February 21, 1883, *War Cry*, there was a report that the Captain was fined for obstruction in the Market Place. He refused to pay the fine and had the threat of a fourteen-day sentence hanging over his head. The second of these two reports which was found in the March

---

[34] London *War Cry*. June 18, 1882.
[35] London *War Cry*. July 27, 1882.

21, 1883, *War Cry* probably involved other members of the Bach/Goodchild family for Margaret and Richard's parents had become Salvationists.

SEVEN DAYS FOR JESUS

> This week has been one of real happiness to our souls. Though they cast our Captain into prison, God led us on. The devil is raging in all shapes and forms in this town, but in spite of all opposition we mean to push the battle to the gates. Grand day on Sunday; open-air good all day. Just got to the Barracks at night when up came a Policeman who took the names of three of us for marching and singing through the streets. Captain Margetts, A. D. O. [Assistant Divisional Officer], was with us all day. We finished up with one soul. On Monday, our Captain's time being up, we had a grand demonstration at night. We had the A. D. O. and two Lieutenants, with about ninety soldiers and brass band, from Reading. We met them at the station, mounted our Captain on a pony, and away we went with a howling mob after us. We only got half round the town when the devil began to rage. The road was blocked but still on we went, the town being all in an uproar.

HAND-TO-HAND FIGHT FOR THE COLORS.

> The devil's agents came upon us, about five to one, to try to get the colors. The staff broke in the middle, but we sprang forward and got the colors around our arms, as we brought them off the battle-field with only a slight injury. Although the Soldiers were knocked about, not a blow was returned. No protection from the police. We reached our Barracks after a time which were packed.[36]

This story is significant since, according to family lore, our step-great grandfather, Robert Goodchild, became the color sergeant and may have been involved in this mêlée as well as our great grandmother and others of the family. An interesting sidelight in this report was that Captain Margetts accompanied them that day. This name will reappear later in this narration. He will have a direct impact on Margaret and Richard's ministries some years later.

---

[36] London *War Cry*. Mar. 21, 1883.

This was the atmosphere into which Richard and Margaret Bach came, and it was no surprise that she became one of hundreds of new converts. She and her brother became enthusiastic Salvationists. She used to say that on Sunday the two of them left early enough to walk, first to Reading and later to Wokingham. They attended all of the activities of the day and walked home after the last amen of the evening.

When did Margaret and Richard feel the calling to become Salvation Army officers? Edward Higgins, future General of The Salvation Army and an earlier acquaintance in Reading, stated that "while attending the opening of the Clapton Congress Hall as well as the Army's first demonstration at the Alexandria Palace in August, Higgins resolved to apply for officership.[37] London was not that far away and it was the custom in those days to obtain special fares from the railroad and arrange train excursions to special events. It is probable that they were in attendance also. Was it on one of these occasions that Richard and Margaret also made their decision to enter training for officership? This would agree with what Margaret is quoted as saying, "You know in those days, you got your ticket of acceptance one day and entered the Training Home the next."[38] They began their training on September 7, 1882.

---

[37] Harris, William. *Storm Pilot*: The story of the life of General Edward Higgins. London: The Salvation Army. 1981. p. 17.
[38] Canadian *War Cry*. Jan. 5, 1925. p. 6.

CHAPTER FIVE

Preparing For The Battle

". . . beaten, yet not killed . . . ."
II Corinthians 6:9 NIV

For Margaret, going to the training home meant separation for the first time from her mother, stepfather and younger Goodchild step siblings. She and her brother, Richard William, were entering into a new world of unchartered waters. The Army was still very new and not many had given their lives to this "upstart" organization. What would the future hold?

There was little formal structure in the beginning. Everything in The Salvation Army was still in a state of flux. The only training for officers consisted of acceptance of the candidate and placing him or her under the apprenticeship of an officer in a corps, and with time they received an appropriate rank. In addition, a number of training depots were set up around the United Kingdom where the cadets trained in small groups. An important development took place in 1875 when, for the first time, a woman was entrusted with the leadership of a "station." That honor belonged to Annie Davis. Since she was successful, this practice continued as "The Army was formed."[39] This custom originated in 1880 when it was perceived that women should receive some relevant training, so the house that had been the Booth family home was remodeled to accommodate thirty women. Since this

---

[39] Walker, Pamela J. *Pulling the Devil's Kingdom Down*. Berkely: University of California Press. 2001. p. 56.

plan proved to be very successful, it was decided that the same arrangement should be made for the men, and a house was obtained for this reason. The leadership for these two programs was given to Emma Booth and Ballington Booth. Late in 1881 the opportunity to purchase the large "London Orphan Asylum" presented itself, and an appeal went out to Salvationists and friends to help raise the necessary funds to do so. Both men and women were trained in this building, but their programs, for the most part, would remain separate. The name for that building became Clapton Congress Hall.[40] On September 7, 1882, Margaret and Richard arrived there for their training.

Booth shared some thoughts about the content of this program.

> Some friends have been a little afraid that we are in danger of departing from the simplicity of the movement, and going off on to college lines. They must come and see us, and their fears will at once vanish. In these homes we propose:
>
> 1) to test the genuineness of the candidate; 2) we teach the outlines of Bible history and doctrine, with something of reading, writing and spelling; 3) we give some instruction in home and personal habits; 4) we train in house-to-house visitation, street work, indoor meetings, and all the measures peculiar to the Army; 5) we seek to develop and encourage and confirm the uttermost devotion to God, and for self-sacrifice for the salvation of men.[41]

The period of training was just a matter of weeks. Because a future general, Edward Higgins, from Reading, was a member of the same group of cadets along with Margaret and Richard William, we have some details that otherwise would have been lost. The opening day of their (cadets') session was Thursday, September 7, 1882. The biography of General Higgins states,

> . . . but the hurly-burly of training, with its emphasis on practice rather than theory, helped him. In common with cadets of the 1880s he had many unpleasant experiences, especially in connection with open-air evangelism. The Salvation Army waged its unrelenting war against sin and many were the vicious counter-attacks by the forces of evil. It was a rough business. The cadets were frequently attacked by the mob. Clothes were spoiled

---

[40] Sandall. Vol. II. p. 67.
[41] Sandall. Vol. II. p. 68.

and black eyes and physical injuries were common. Sometimes the rowdies prevented the cadets marching and on occasions they had to cover their uniforms in order to reach Clapton [the training home] in safety.[42]

It was on one of these occasions that Margaret's tambourine was snatched from her hands. It was a common practice of those in the skeleton army (a group organized by the liquor interests to oppose the Salvationists) to try to grab anything from the Salvationists while they were on the march. The tambourine was Margaret's prized possession as it had been presented to her at the time she left Wokingham to enter the training home. There was an inscription on the skin, "Prepare to Meet Thy God." Some weeks later, it was returned by the "thief" to the training home, rather the worse for wear, with an apology along with the confession that it had been the instrument of his salvation. Margaret always considered him her first convert.[43]

Although the men and women were trained in separate programs, it is likely that they were united in one place when General William Booth or the Army Mother Catherine Booth came to speak. Higgins observed as follows: "Outstanding in the training home curriculum were lectures and 'spiritual days' by General William Booth and the Army Mother, [Mrs. Catherine Booth]."

He further stated that he learned the secret of prayer from the practical lectures on the subject by Catherine Booth.

> He said concerning a day of extreme discouragement: Such light came to me as she spoke. She talked on lines which comforted me; made me anxious to pray for a deeper love for souls and to be willing to sacrifice if only I might become a soul-winner . . . . I remember so well as the lecture closed I went up to my dormitory and settled the question, deciding in my heart as never before, 'Come what may, I am going through.'[44]

Undoubtedly, Margaret Bach and her brother Richard William received the benefit of these kinds of experiences. Years later when interviewed by The Canadian *War Cry*, January 5, 1929, Margaret recalled some of her experiences during those weeks at the training home which agree with Edward Higgins'

---

[42] Harris. p. 1-17.
[43] Edwin & Elsie Payton and Flossie Holder. Recorded interview. 1983.
[44] Harris. p. 17.

memory. She recalled the fact that she attended the wedding of Bramwell Booth which took place in the same building as the training home.

A Rough Sketch of the Wedding Scene at Clapton, 12th October, 1882.

The wedding of Bramwell and Florence Booth.
Courtesy of The Salvation Army International Heritage Center, London, England.

Margaret talked about the opposition of "the skeleton army" that used to march in front of them carrying a flag and hearing their vulgar songs as well as the weight of their missiles as they bombarded the Army open-air meetings. Perhaps her clearest memory was that of the official opening of The Eagle and The Grecian.

As mentioned in chapter two, the Eagle was a public house (tavern) and the Grecian was a theater and dance hall. There was a famous ditty which was sung for many years as follows:

Up and down the City Road
In and out the Eagle;
That's the way the money goes,
Pop goes the weasel!

What is implied in this parody is that this public house attracted people who were so addicted to alcohol that they had pawned (popped) their watches (weasels) in order to continue their drinking. The liquor industry raised a huge opposition to the purchase of the lease for this facility by The Salvation Army. This was first unsuccessfully attempted in the courts and then by a mob of 30,000 people. Margaret describes the situation:

> The Founder secured the lease of this den of iniquity and prepared to turn it into a center of Army activity. This move stirred the opposition of the very worst of London roughs and serious rioting occurred at the opening. It was a day to be remembered by the Cadets. We were arrayed in special uniforms of the coarsest material, and before leaving the Training Home the roll was called and we were told we must not go unless we were ready to lay down our lives, and it was fully expected that some of us would be killed. Faced with such a challenge, of course we all went. When we reached 'The Grecian,' we were battered and bruised and covered from head to foot with filth of all kinds, but nobody was killed. When it was time to go home, a message was received from police headquarters that the Cadets were not to leave the building until a detachment of police could be sent from Scotland Yard. By a bit of strategy, the police held most of the mob in a cross street while the Cadets went home another way and escaped much of the violence. The newspapers said that the roughs were in such a frenzy that when they were cheated of their prey, they used their missiles on each other.[45]

---

[45] Canadian *War Cry*. Jan. 5, 1929. p. 6.

The Eagle Tavern.[46]

The women cadets marched arm in arm in the middle of the group and the men marched on the outside in order to receive the worst of the onslaught of missiles. Cadet Higgins later recalled the same event which happened in their first month of training,

> In September 1882 William Booth acquired the notorious Grecian Theatre in Hoxton, London, when 6000 people crowded to the first day's meetings. These were occasions of fierce opposition—both inside and outside the building; but often in the midst of the most unbecoming tumult the Penitent-form would be lined again and again with many of the people who had come to disturb. These were memorable moments for the young man who had been attracted to the Army by its soul-saving zeal.[47]

---

[46] Sandall, Vol. II. p. 213
[47] Harris. p. 17.

In the service of dedication William Booth commenced his remarks as follows:

> 'So you've got through.' I remarked to a sister as she wriggled through the last few lines of the enemy and grasped my hand at the gate. 'Oh, we are always bound to get through,' was the characteristic reply, and I could not help thinking how much the remark and the whole circumstances hit off the real march of the Army. It has always been to get "through" something. Difficulties upon difficulties seem to be piled up; but after all they do not, cannot, stop us. How could there be so hostile a crowd? We shall know all about that very soon. We are capturing persons from amongst them, thank God, at every service, and they will tell us all the secrets bye-an-bye.[48]

In another message in a later meeting of the day he said this:

> A merchant said to one of my Officers in Leicester, 'Can't you stop this going on in the open-air during the winter: some of your people will get cold?' He replied, 'I will stop the open-air preaching if you will stop the people dying, but while the people are dying and going to hell, we must try and preach and stop them.'[49]

Although the training period was limited in time, cadets of this group were exposed to several unique experiences. While Margaret was there, the founder of The Salvation Army in France "La Marechale" Catherine Booth (daughter of the founder) and a group of her helpers as well as new converts conducted a service to a huge crowd in the Clapton Congress Hall. The cadets were present and participated. Several of the young converts shared their experiences of having their lives radically changed when they accepted the Lord's salvation. When one considers that the pioneers had only "opened fire" in Paris in March 1881, a short year and a half prior to this meeting, one can imagine the enthusiasm exhibited on this occasion.[50]

Without a doubt, life at The Training Home was frugal. Many steps were taken by faith in those days without the clear assurance of the finances to accomplish them. The following announcement would appear periodically in

---

[48] London *War Cry*. Sept. 30, 1882.
[49] London *War Cry*. Sept. 30, 1882.
[50] London *War Cry*. Oct. 21, 1882.

the *War Cry* magazines. "This can only be done (sending out new officers) in proportion as the Lord opens the hearts of those who love and believe in the work of The Salvation Army to make a real self-denying effort to enable us to meet the needs of the homes."

> What can you do to help us?
> We need meat, fish, vegetables, groceries, dairy products, etc. Can you give these, or can you supply us with them at an exceptionally low rate for the work's sake? We need clothes, boots, etc., and we are very heavily pressed for money.[51]

In the Christmas edition of the 1882 *War Cry,* a woman cadet was asked to give her impressions of life as a cadet. It gives us an additional impression of what life was like for Margaret Bach:

> I think we are a very happy lot of girls. The first law and rule of our Home is loving one another, and this is not a rule that is kept just when it is convenient, but a positive law, observed at all times, and everywhere, in the housework, in the schoolroom, at the wash-tub . . . . There is a wonderful "Christ" influence in our Home. It seems as if Jesus walks about there in a special manner, and teaches every girl Himself as some precious charges . . . . Sometimes when we are out visiting, a woman will come to the door and directly she catches sight of the Hallelujah bonnet, will just stop to scream out as much abuse as she can get in half a minute, and then bang the door to again not stopping to hear our lassies, quiet, 'The Lord bless you, ma'am:' but this is not always the case. Some of the poor people (for we go to the very poorest houses), receive us gratefully, and listen as we speak to them of God and their souls' Salvation, sometimes till the tears run down their faces, and they show that the Saviour has spoken to their hearts, then the thing is to get them to the Savior's feet . . . . We have hard work *War Cry* selling. We have to trudge up and down a great many steps to sell a few; but then, as Miss Booth says, 'It will make good soldiers of us.'

Today the commissioning of new officers is one of the outstanding events on the annual calendar of The Salvation Army. Since cadets were coming out of The Training Home several times a year in the early 1800s, they did

---

[51] Londo*n War Cry.* May 1885.

not have a formal commissioning ceremony. For Margaret and Richard, something occurred precisely at the time they were to conclude their training. Their "commissioning" became an event that is recorded in the official history of the organization. The growth of the Army was rapid and the need was urgent to send reinforcements to foreign lands as well as additional officers to commence the work in new countries. There was an announcement of the "Commissioning of the 101" to be held in Exeter Hall, an auditorium that held three-thousand people on November 28, 1882.

Cadets Passing the Bank of England and Royal Exchange on their way to Exeter Hall.

Courtesy, The Salvation Army International Heritage Center, London, England.

It was to be a colorful all-day affair with meetings in the morning, afternoon and evening. Whereas in the meetings for the dedication of The Eagle and The Grecian, the Founder and Mrs. Booth spoke of the rapid growth and the acquisition of about ten buildings during 1882. In these meetings the emphasis was on the Salvationists' responsibility to evangelize the world. There were flags from the nations where some of the officers were going, and in some cases, special uniforms appropriate to their countries were shown. As each group of officers going to another country to either open fire or to reinforce the work, a Salvation Army flag was presented to the group by different members of the Booth family. On that occasion officers were to be sent to the United States, Canada and India where the work had been established for only a short time. Others were sent to Sweden, South Africa and New Zealand to establish the work. On the same platform there were fifty men and thirty-six women cadets who were being sent out into the British field, some to open thirty-nine new corps.[52] The reason we are certain that Margaret and Richard William were in that group is the following December 7 *War Cry,* report: "The General pointed to a brother and sister saved out of one family who were going to South Wales."[53] We have not been able to confirm Richard William's first appointment. Margaret Elizabeth's first three appointments were in South Wales. On December 23, 1882, Margaret Elizabeth arrived at the town of Brynmawr in South Wales, and that is another story. Before we leave the famous commissioning of the 101, here is an interesting anecdote.

> Captain Elizabeth Pellett later Mrs. Jacob Styles, then stationed at Wokingham [Corps from where Margaret and Richard departed to attend the training home], was called to attend the meeting, but was surprised indeed when she was told at the door of the hall that she was among the four to go to America—a telegram containing her overseas orders had not reached her. It is characteristic of the spirit of the times that the Captain had no thought of questioning her orders although her obedience involved her sailing [the] next day. In the U. S. A. the captain had a stirring career, pioneering at Louisville, Kentucky, and Asbury Park, New Jersey.[54]

---

[52] London *War Cry.* Dec. 2, 7, 1882.
[53] London *War Cry.* Dec. 9, 1882.
[54] Sandall. Vol. II. p. 223.

Chapter Six

On to the Conflict

"On to the conflict, soldier, for the right,
Arm you with the Spirit's sword and march to fight;
Truth be your watchword, sounding the ringing cry:
Victory, victory, victory!"
   William Howard Doanne (1832-1915) Salvation Army Songbook

Brynmawr

With the fanfare of the great meeting with three thousand in attendance in Exeter Hall behind her, sometime in December Margaret was met by Captain Agnes H. Anthony, her future corps officer. She was a large Negro woman from the United States, and together they proceeded to the train station for the trip to her first appointment.

When they were seated on the train, Captain Anthony discovered that she had been pick-pocketed. Their train tickets were gone as well as all their money except two pennies. How they managed to continue on their journey is a mystery, but they arrived in Brynmawr on December 23, 1882.[55] Brynmawr was a coal mining town, an industry which at that time was important for building the economy including exportation. They found that the corps had been without officers for a period of time but that the local officers (lay

---

[55] Canadian *War Cry*. Jan. 5, 1929.

leaders) had been carrying on the ministry.[56] Margaret remembered that their first meeting was on a rainy evening, and the roof leaked so badly that the congregation used their umbrellas to keep from getting wet. They quickly launched into their responsibilities, and God blessed their efforts as can be seen by reports from The *War Cry*.[57]

> Private Thomas Jones writes:—The new Officers arrived on Saturday. Sunday, meetings grand all day. Three sinners professed to have found peace during the day. Christmas Day, all rejoicing; five souls came on the Lord's side. All the week-night meetings wonderfully owned and blessed of God. Saturday night, forty in the procession.[58]
>
> The 111th [Corps] "Blood-and-Fire" Soldiers are marching under the command of Captain Anthony and Lieutenant Bach. After a month's hard fighting and pleading for Brynmawr, God is giving us the victory. Twenty-eight have been redeemed since their arrival. One of the prisoners has been the biggest drunkard in Brynmawr, praise the Lord! He is working for Jesus now. The devil is losing some of his stolen property. One woman said last week that she was so thankful that her husband had given God his heart, for when he was serving the devil and drinking he used to make her sing the devil's songs, but now she is singing God's praises in the Old Pavillion. [The Royal Pavillion was the largest building in the town.] . . . The Lord has been with us during the last week, and he has been manifesting His presence powerfully in the Salvation of souls. One of our sisters farewelled at night for the Training Home. She gave a very earnest, touching appeal to the unsaved. We had a grand Holiness Meeting on Friday, when all the soldiers went in for more of the Holy Ghost. Last Sunday night the Devil was kicking in our meeting, but, praise the Lord, he lost two of his agents, and now they are drinking of the fountain of life freely.
> Thomas Jones, for Captain Anthony[59]

---

[56] London *War Cry*. Dec. 30, 1882.
[57] Canadian *War Cry*. Jan. 5, 1929.
[58] London *War Cry*. Jan. 10, 1883.
[59] London *War Cry*. Aug. 22, 1883.

Lieutenant Bach writes:

> The devil is raging, and Jesus is raising. Sunday, good meetings all day. We began at seven in the morning. God was with us, Soldiers came up well. Deep conviction all day. Monday night, good open-air meeting. We marched to our Hall believing God would save souls. Bless Him! He did not disappoint us. When we gave the invitation three souls came to Jesus and found pardon, one of them being the worst character in Brynmawr.[60]

A special event took place in the town of Merthyr Tydfil which was just seven miles away and was to be Margaret's second appointment. General William Booth visited there.

The *War Cry* reported the following:

> Merthyr was besieged on Thursday. From an early hour the members of The Salvation Army forces were on the alert and soon train after train poured in troops of soldiers eager to take part in the assault which was about to be made on the inhabitants. The Company stationed at Merthyr is not very strong; but as the ranks were swelled by contingents from the Rhondda Valley quite an imposing appearance was presented . . . . When The Founder's special train arrived at 2:35 P. M. there were thousands awaiting him and there was a grand procession to the Drill Hall where two meetings were held.[61]

Without a doubt Margaret was present in that throng of people, another of the several times that she had the privilege of being under the ministry of William Booth.

Merthyr Tydfil

Margaret arrived at her second appointment on June 21, 1883, as the assistant officer to Captain Kate Henderson in the southwestern Welsh town of Merthyr Tydfil.

---

[60] London *War Cry*. Feb. 21, 1883.
[61] London *War Cry*. May 12, 1883.

Lieutenant Maggie Bach writes:

> MERTHYR TYDFIL (Capt. Kate Henderson)
> We are still going up. God is blessing us in a wonderful manner and souls are being saved. In our Free-and-Easy [meeting] on Sunday afternoon one brother said before he was saved he thought nothing of going into a public-house and drinking seven quarts of beer, but now he is drinking at the Fountain. Another man who was saved a week ago told us what a vile sinner he had been, but now he was saved and trusting in Jesus, Hallelujah! We mean victory through the Blood.[62]

This is the only report available of her time in Merthyr Tydfil. In November she was appointed to assist Captain Henderson in another southwestern town of Wales.

Trelaw

It is interesting to read the Salvation Army language of the day (November 1883) through the one report from Margaret concerning her time in Trelaw.

> Glory, Hallelujah! We are still marching on to war at Trelaw. The past week has been one of hard fighting with sin and the devil, but we had victory through the Blood. Sunday was a good day. We met at seven in the morning for Knee-drill [prayer meeting]. The Heavenly light came down and flooded our souls. Our faith ran high for a good day. Good Holiness Meeting at eleven. At two o'clock we met for open-air at Pen-y-graig. After a good meeting our brass band marched off playing, "Oh! the voice to me so dear."
>
> Inside, our Free-and-Easy [meeting] was grand as one after another testified to the saving power of God through the precious blood of Jesus, but our night meeting was the crowning time. Lieutenant David Davis was with us from Penzance, and after the Captain gave the invitation four came to the Saviour and found pardon through the Blood.
>
> Lieutenant Maggie Bach, for Captain Kate Henderson.[63]

---

[62] London *War Cry*. Oct. 10, 1883.
[63] London *War Cry*. Dec. 15, 1883.

It is revealing to sense Margaret's earnestness and zeal as she wrote these reports. It should be remembered that she was a relatively new believer, had only a grammar school education and only fourteen weeks of preparation in her Training Home experience. She demonstrated a total commitment to the salvation of the lost, something that prevailed among the early Salvationists.

Chapter Seven

Continuing the Conflict

*"With salvation for every nation,
To the ends of the earth we will go.
With a free and full salvation,
All the power of the cross we'll show."*

William James Person (1832-1892)
Salvation Army Songbook

YORKSHIRE

There are no other reports of Margaret's time in South West Wales. According to her memory, she was stationed in that division for fifteen months. She was stationed in additional corps as will become apparent later. From Wales she was sent to assist another officer, and together they opened a corps in the town of Goole in the Yorkshire Division.

Town of Goole

On March 22, 1884, Lieutenant Margaret Bach arrived along with Captain Emily Argyle to the town of Goole. They were obviously using a rented building (Market Hall)[64] because it was not available two nights a

---

[64] London *War Cry*. May 7, 1884.

week.[65] As was the custom then, there were meetings every evening so on those nights they held open-air services. God blessed their efforts as they reported several outstanding cases of salvation as the following example illustrates:

> One converted infidel said that three weeks ago he came to our meeting to pull us to pieces but, thank God, He pulled him to pieces. Another man said he had been the biggest sinner in Goole. Had not been in the House of God for years; but he came into The Salvation Army Market Hall, fell at the feet of Jesus, gave up sin and the devil, and is now rejoicing in a sin-pardoning God.[66]

Town of Huddersfield

The narration of this book begins with the experience that Margaret Bach faced in Huddersfield when the Infidel Society threatened to refute whatever the officer read from the Bible in the Sunday evening service. This was to be her first experience in leading a corps. The corps was opened in March or April of 1883, and from the start there was the usual opposition as reported in the London *War Cry*.[67] Margaret arrived at her new appointment on November 6, 1884.

> After our Sunday victories we went down to Castlegate, the roughest part of the town. The rough[s] set upon us, and carried us completely away with them. We got kicked about a good deal and our drum was broken, but, best of all, we got our Hall packed and captured one soul for Jesus.[68]

Apparently reporting on the same riot we read:

> Captain Ellen Ashworth in command, assisted by the reserves and a few natives who have been captured in battle, have marched into the trenches of the enemy, and while passing down one street, heavy firing from the enemy commenced. Grape [a type of ammunition] and canister flew about the heads of our comrades in the shape of stones and rubbish. Then the devil rushed out all his forces from

---

[65] London *War Cry*. Mar. 5, 1884.
[66] London *War Cry*. Apr. 12, 1884.
[67] London *War Cry*. Apr. 4, 1883.
[68] London *War Cry*. Apr. 11, 1883.

their strongholds and scattered our Soldiers, kicking and punching with terrific violence. Black Tommy was kicked about like a football, and his kettle-drum was taken from him and tossed in the air, but was recaptured. The big drum was broken, and had it not been for the assistance of the police, more serious would have been the wounds received in the conflict. Bugler Foster was taken to the doctor and had his wounds dressed, but wounded as our Soldiers were, on they went to the Barracks, which was crowded inside and out, and at the close of the day prisoners were captured and great rejoicings were in our camp.[69]

In spite of the persecution or as a result of it, crowds were attracted so it was necessary on Sunday evenings to rent the Armory. We have not been able to ascertain how many people it held, but we know that the corps "barracks" normally held five hundred people, and on one occasion seven hundred people were crammed into the building. This would indicate that the Armory was much larger than the barracks. It is no wonder that Margaret was concerned when she was warned of the confrontation from the infidels that was to come on that fateful Sunday evening.[70] Following this rigorous appointment it appears that she either had a short period of rest or she was given a less stressful one for she again served as an assistant officer.

Town of Yeadon

It appears that she enjoyed a longer stay in Goole than in other assignments because we know that she went to Yeadon in March of 1885. Here she assisted Captain Emily Argyle.[71]

The only report on Margaret's activities in Yeadon is found in an article she wrote for the London *War Cry*.

> A SUCCESSFUL CAMPAIGN AT YEADON
> Sunday was a good day; one sinner sought and found the Saviour. On Monday we were reinforced by the Dewsbury and Huddersfield brass bands [Huddersfield was her previous appointment] and a host of Soldiers who did much damage to the devil's kingdom. In the afternoon the Captain took them and bombarded the

---

[69] London *War Cry*. Apr. 21, 1883.
[70] London *War Cry*. Feb. 6, 1884.
[71] London *War Cry*. Mar. 11, 1885.

villages round, bringing the people out and making them think of Salvation.

After a good tea of ham, cake, and tarts, we met for a triumphant march, after which we parted and held three open airs at once. The Huddersfield brass band was on Penny Fort Hill and the Dewsbury band was on the Green. It stirred the whole town. Inside we held an indescribable meeting. Some wonderful testimonies were given by the Soldiers of each Corps and at a quarter-past nine we closed one of the best days we ever spent for Jesus. Lieutenant Maggie Bach, for Captain Emily Argyle. [72]

Town of Filey

On July 29, 1885, Margaret received her promotion to Captain and an appointment to be in charge of the Filey Corps. Filey is on the northeast coast of the country thus you will see the use of sea terms in the reports that appear in the London *War Cry*. From the January 28, 1885, *War Cry*, prior to her arrival, there is an example of this, "The fishermen of Filey the other night helped to sing eight sinners into the sea of God´s love and forgetfulness of sin."[73] The following reports are from her time there.

> Victory! Victory! Souls and Glory!
> God indeed has been blessing us of late. Our building used to be nearly empty, but it now gets filled with just the right sort, whom we believe God will save very soon.
>
> We had a special "Go" on Saturday and Sunday among all classes, and our comrades, the Wesleyans, well to the front. God bless them! We had a children's tea, 313 sat down to gain the victory, which they did. Then a public tea and Salvation Jubilee—building full, rapt attention.
>
> Sunday, a red-letter day here, wonderful power and liberty; open-airs beyond description. The fish-lads help us wonderfully, as to the beat of our favorite big drum they rouse the town with their singing. God bless and save them!

---

[72] London *War Cry*. July 18, 1885.
[73] London *War Cry*. July 18, 1885.

Inside, wonderful attention, marvelous liberty. As a brother spoke at night, the people were broken down, and best of all, two souls. Hallelujah! "May God keep them faithful!" is the prayer of Uncle Jack.[74]

The fight is hard, but we shall win; with Jack and Jack's wife for a procession, we dare go forward in the lanes and alleys of Filey to lift up Jesus, the Sinner's Friend. We felt it good to stand almost alone for God, for He stood by our side.

A few people came inside the Barracks, and we had liberty. The Spirit was in the word. Filey shall yet rise; God does not forget it.[75]

There followed a series of appointments for which we have been able to obtain little or no information with the exception of the dates of her appointments in addition to one photograph. They are:

Kirkby Foley

She was appointed there on October 1885.

Bristol VII

On January 30, 1886, she took command of this corps and this photograph confirms her presence there.

---

[74] London *War Cry*. Dec. 16, 1885.
[75] London *War Cry*. Feb. 20, 1886.

Lieutenant Greenwood, Captain Margaret Bach, Annie Dunsbury.

Chippaham

Her appointment here dates from April 25, 1886.

Runcorn

In spite of the fact that she held this appointment for what would have been considered a lengthy stay in those days, we do not have any information of her time there from January 13, 1887, until she arrived at her next corps on December 29 of that same year.

THE BLACK COUNTRY

Margaret stated in the January 25, 1929, Canadian *War Cry* that she was appointed to the Black Country, a term used for a certain area of the country. It received this title because it was an industrial and manufacturing area in middle England. The tag of Black Country denoted the heavy industrial use of coal in smelting furnaces. This speaks to us of the period of the Industrial Revolution when little thought was given to the environment.

Captain Margaret Bach and Lieutenant Eveline Shepperd.

Stafford

We next find Margaret Bach in what perhaps was her most serious challenge. Although not aware of it when appointed to the town of Stafford, she was sent to open the corps. She arrived on December 29, 1887. There was no building or apartment awaiting her. In addition no landlord would rent her a house until the mayor issued a guarantee against property damage by the roughs. She secured a building in the lowest section of the town; the windows opened onto a cemetery and her entire stock of furniture consisted of her trunk and a small teapot. Later Lieutenant Shepperd, an assistant, arrived. They rented a theater for Sunday meetings and things began to happen. The crowds were enormous, jamming the theater to the doors for every meeting, but the state of order was terrible. She would start the crowd singing, but could not stop them; they would sing until they were exhausted.

When the novelty had worn off this form of amusement, the troublemakers tried rougher tactics. A gang stood up in the gallery and yelled every time she tried to speak. Margaret took the case to court after she learned the name of the ringleader only to have it thrown out. The feeling was so bitter that she had to be escorted from the courtroom by the police. The chief held the crowd in check by the cryptic warning when he said, "If you show your teeth, I'll make you bite your tongues."

The next move was so serious that the roughs were defeated by their own mischievous activities. A young man began to put out the lights and cry "fire." He was stopped in time to prevent a panic, but the landlord demanded that he be prosecuted. It turned out that he was the only son of a widow, and Margaret promised to spare him on condition that he make a public apology from the platform the following Sunday. He did so, and it was such a humiliation for him that the crowd had second thoughts about any further disturbance. After that she achieved peace and order.[76]

Stafford was the county seat where a jail was located. The officers often held open-air meetings outside the jail for the benefit of those incarcerated inside. Margaret made it a point to hold the open air meetings at this site for their benefit. Some Salvationists from other corps had been jailed for such charges as obstructing traffic and disturbing the peace. She was eventually warned by the local newspaper that, if she wasn't careful, rather than being on the outside looking in, she would be on the inside looking out. At the corps, the opposition was so fierce that following their meetings at the end of the day, the soldiers and friends made it a point to leave in large groups so as to be able to defend themselves. On one occasion when they opened the door to leave, they saw two rows of policemen outside facing away from the center to protect them from the refuse expected to be thrown from the Skeleton Army.[77]

There are several articles from that period that confirm Margaret's claim to have been the officer who opened that corps. When she was in a position to schedule the official opening, she invited the divisional staff to help. The Divisional Officer submitted a report to the *War Cry* following that effort.

---

[76] Canadian *War Cry*. Jan. 5, 1929.
[77] Payton, Edwin. Personal recorded interview about conversations with his mother. 1983.

OPENING OF STAFFORD

Our first appearance created a great amount of curiosity. Having secured the Lyceum Theatre, a building accommodating some 800 or 900 people, we arrived on Saturday, accompanied by eight or nine specials. After giving out handbills we took our stand in the market-place, and before the first verse was sung hundreds gathered around. God enabled us to deal out salvation, and a quack doctor was bewildered, having lost all his congregation. Around Sunday's open-air meetings crowds gathered to hear the message of mercy. Inside, 300 or 400 had gathered at our first meeting; a most wonderful time was spent. One young fellow, who I was told was the biggest scamp in the town, sought and found mercy. Afternoon, place packed. We had a little rowdyism from a few of the "mashers," but God took hold of the people, and they found that after all we were not theatrical folks, but people of God and not until close upon five o'clock could we close the meeting. Hall packed out again at night, hundreds outside unable to get in. We did not close the first part of the meeting until quarter to nine; the people were riveted to their seats. A tremendous struggle at the wind-up; only one openly evidenced conversion, but many a heart was smitten, and we are believing for a great ingathering of souls. The police were extremely kind and helped us well. God bless them.

Major Noyce [78]

Life on the Stage at Stafford.
The new D. O. [Divisional Officer] and Lydia, the junior soldier songster, received a warm reception in the open-air on Saturday. Amid the row we were able to pour out truth that made sinners feel wretched. We marked changes in their expressions and tones of language. The barracks were filled before we reached them. While testimonies were freely and heartily given by many who only a few weeks ago were enslaved by drink and sin of all kinds, our hopes and expectations for a good day on Sunday strengthened. Good time at knee-drill. Our marches, stands and indoor meetings were times of power and blessings, despite the few who were enslaved by the drink.

---

[78] London *War Cry.* Jan. 7, 1888.

Breathless attention in the packed theatre at night. One young woman came on the stage, where she sought and found salvation. When we were about to close another settled the question for eternity. During the week twenty-one sought pardon, the result we believe of Sunday's struggles. The junior soldiers' work has been commenced. In the first meeting a little lad knelt at the penitent-form for pardon. Hallelujah! The devil rages, but we are sure to win. Our cry is 'Stafford for our crucified, but now highly exalted Lord.'
Capt. Bach and Lieut. Evaline Shepperd[79]

Stafford, the county town, the jail town, the town of painful discipline, the town which has just been invaded by the Lord's Salvation Army was the place of our third visit. We are confident of producing a marked change in the town, and of decreasing the number of pent-up jail birds. We had a lively time in the open air, and Captain Herbert Curtis, the Divisional Scribe, told of God's power to save young respectables as well as besotted drunkards. In the barracks, which was packed, we had the joy of seeing seven cry for mercy. Captain Bach and Lieutenant Shepperd (lass[i]es) are having victory all around, and a bright Corps is in course of manufacture.[80]

Stafford
Since our arrival here, some of the worst sinners in the town have been reclaimed. One of our converts before he was saved said, 'Why if I were to join you, you would have no more to do in Stafford; I am the worst fellow in the town.' He is now a most promising soldier and recognizes that there is yet a great deal to be done.[81]

There appears to be a gap here which we have not yet been able to fill. Perhaps Margaret once again needed a time of rest and recuperation. According to family lore we have been told that she was in Hanley which is famous in The Salvation Army history because Gipsy Smith was dismissed from the Army from there. It is obvious that was not the case. However, she was quite close to Hanley when she was in Stafford. The only evidence we

---

[79] London *War Cry*. Feb. 25, 1888.
[80] London *War Cry*. Feb. 4, 1888.
[81] London *War Cry*. May 19, 1888.

have of Margaret being there is a photograph of her with one other which has the name of the photography studio in Hanley written on the back.

Town of Leek

Margaret arrived in the town of Leek on June 19, 1888, her last appointment in England.[82]

We know of only one minor problem Margaret had to contend with there. The corps did not previously have a drum nor did they want one. However, she acquired one to play herself. When she did persuade a soldier to play it, he was promptly arrested for disturbing the peace.

The approximate date of her departure from Leek is confirmed by the dedication on the flyleaf of a book titled *The Land and the Book* by Reverend W. M. Thompston which was presented to her on the occasion of her farewell. The inscription reads, "Presented by G. S. Mears to Miss Bach on her departure from Leek with tokens of respect. March 12, 1889."

The Salvation Army was experiencing substantial growth in the United States, and there was a need for qualified leadership. Margaret was asked if she would be willing to take an appointment there since she was an American citizen. She consented to undertake this major change, and at the age of twenty-six, made plans to begin the journey which would open an entirely new and challenging transformation in her life that would include meeting the Payton Family.

---

[82] Canadian *War Cry.* Jan. 5, 1829.

Chapter Eight

A New Life in a New World

> *The Lord had said to Abram, "Leave your country, your people and your father's household and go to the land I will show you."*
> Genesis 12:1 NIV

Bath, England, County of Somerset, is the home of many Payton families. We were able to trace one family back for five generations in our search, though it was not possible to link them to our tree. Three Payton families living in Bath were contacted in 2011, but no new information was learned about the William Payton branch. In 1998 two of William's great great grandsons visited Bath and noted a long list of Paytons in the telephone book.

The name of our great grandfather was discovered only through recent research. His name was not known in oral history or recorded family history. In the Little Lake Cemetery Registry, (Peterborough Ontario), the information for the burial of his son, Edward Henry, listed his father's name as "Father Payton" and his mother's name as "Don't know." A great great grandson purchased a copy of Edward's wedding Registry and discovered three facts about Edward's father; his name was William, his occupation was gardener, and he was deceased by 1863. Very recently, and with the help of the ancestral records of The Church of the Latter Day Saints, it was discovered that Edward was christened on January 29, 1838. That source also provided the name of William's wife, Susan.

Knowing something of the history of Bath could help our understanding of the influence the community had on shaping the lives of our ancestors. The name of the city is based on the natural hot springs located in the center of town. Archaeological evidence shows that the spring was treated as a shrine by Iron Age Britons and dedicated to the goddess Sulis. The Romans established Bath in A.D. 43, although it was known as a community previously. A Roman bath and a temple were built A.D. 60-70 and the bathing complex was gradually expanded over the next 300 years.

View in the Roman baths and the cathedral, Bath, England.
Artist, Mark Payton.

Many significant historical events took place at Bath and nearby at Stonehenge:

- It is thought to be the site where King Arthur defeated the Angolo Saxons in 500.
- Edgar was crowned King of England in Bath Abbey in 973.
- The battle of Lansdowne was fought July 1643 on the outskirts of the city.

- In 1676 the the health-giving properties of the hot mineral waters came to the attention of the country, and soon the city was crowded by those seeking the healing waters.

The population of the city reached 40,020 according to the 1801 census, making it one of the largest cities in Britain. William was born about this time and later became a gardener. We are still searching for more information to identify his parents. William met Susan, and a family was established. Their first son Edward Henry Payton was born on January 20, 1834, and was christened in Preston-Plucknett, Somerset County, England. His brothers James and William were born in 1845 and 1850 respectively.

Little is known of the young life of Edward until he married Mary Snow. Our knowledge of their lives in Bath is limited to the birth of children. Mary Jane, their first child, was born in 1858 and was named after her mother. William Henry was born in 1861 and named after his grandfather and father. William Henry died at a very young age in 1864. Another son was born in that same year on April 13. He was William Edward, and he too was named after his grandfather and father. There are conflicting dates for the birth of George Charles. There is documentation for 1866 and 1867, but all records agree that he was born on April 5. With the birth of Alfred James in March 1869 and Edwin (Ted) John in 1871, the English family was complete. They were all given royal names. Another daughter would be born after their move to the "New World."

Life in Bath in the 1870s held little hope for a brighter future. Many families were immigrating to the "New World" believing that they would find opportunities that were not available in the "Old World." Land grants were becoming available in Canada and this enticement motivated many families to immigrate. In 1874 Edward and Mary Payton and their children (Mary Jane, 16; William Edward, 10; George Charles, 8; Alfred James, 5; and Edwin John, 3, began a new chapter and a new life in Canada. (This is an estimated year between the birth of Edwin John, in England, and his younger sister Susie, born in Canada.) They settled in the area around Peterborough, Ontario, where the population of the county and the city was 24,651 and 6,812 respectively.[83] The family's first home was in Lakefield, a small community outside of Peterborough. Later they moved to a farm in Buckhorn which may have been an employment decision. The Wright and Payton Pump factory was located in Peterborough. The 1883 *Peterborough Examiner* described a

---

[83] 1881 National census.

devastating fire that destroyed the plant and told of its relocation. We are not certain that they were related to our branch of the Payton clan.[84]

The Salvation Army opened fire in Canada in May of 1882. It was in a time of fierce opposition to the "free and easy" style of their form of worship. Imagine beginning a new ministry with this type of encouragement: "The hostile criticism from moderate men, and other drawbacks we have alluded to, all go to show the Army as a useful religious movement has seen its best days, and makes it somewhat easy to predict the collapse which is almost certain to overtake it sooner or later." This prognostication concluded a two column editorial in the December 10th 1883 edition of the local newspaper. Lord Shaftsbury speaking of the Army said: "It appears to me as a work of the Devil, who having long tried to render Christianity odious, has changed his tactics and is striving to make it ridiculous." Dr DePressensi thought the "principles represented by The Salvation Army, as set forth in the orders of General Booth, should not be endorsed by Protestant Christians." And Spurgeon spoke still more strongly. He said: "Because they would not hinder anything that promised well, Christian men have borne with much that grieved them: but there is a point beyond which long suffering charity cannot go. That point is nearly reached. Even the most ultra-tolerant must feel that hope has been disappointed, and fear now takes its place." In the same article there was praise for the Army reaching out to the poor. "It cannot be denied that the spiritual destitution of England and to some extent, also of other lands, called for some such movement. Pulpit platitudes and monotonous drawling of crude and undigested ideas and, perhaps, in a few cases, excessive ritualism on the part of the English clergy, worked to widen the chasm and to drive the poor man from the church's doors."[85]

Dignitaries of the Anglican and Roman church seemed to unite in praising the organization and its objectives. Cardinal Manning said of it long since, "So far, then, as it brings men to any truth, even though it be only one truth, such as belief in God, in this evil and unbelieving generation, it is doing a work beyond its own foresight. Looking, as we must, over the spiritual devastation of England, every voice that speaks for God is on our side."[86]

It is most certain that Peterborough was the connection that brought The Salvation Army and the Payton family together. A study of that corps'

---

[84] *The Peterborough Examiner.* Nov. 1, 1883.
[85] *The Peterborough Examiner.* Editorial. May 10, 1883.
[86] *The Peterbough Examiner.* May 10, 1883.

history and outreach ministry will help us to understand the positive impact it made on our family's history.

Second row—Mary, Edwin (Ted), William, George, Jim, First row—Edward, Susie, Mary.

A fast growing "Army" was developing in the city. It was on April 1, 1885, when Captain Willis, Cadet Langtry and Cadet Hart "opened fire" and commenced the work of the "Army." The *War Cry* reports many victories in "the battle for souls."

> Since this station has been opened many sinners of the deepest dye have found their way to the foot of the Cross, and they are not only getting their hearts clean but are getting their mouths clean. Hallelujah! Our dear brother said he could praise God not only with a clean heart, but the Lord had washed away his tobacco. Praise the Lord! Sunday the power of the God was in our minds. One out for Holiness and one out for Salvation, making five for the week. Hallelujah!"[87]

---

[87] Canadian *War Cry*. June 13, 1885.

A month later the *War Cry* reported the source of their power and revival.

> At 7 o'clock we all determined to pick out a certain person to pray for. Our prayers and faith were rewarded. . . . seeing eight precious Souls.[88]

This young Corps' goal was ever expanding, and they picked up the vision of William Booth, "The World For God" as expressed in the Canadian *War Cry*. "Eight for Salvation, five for Sanctification. Victory is our motto. We are fighting in the strength of God, and kicking the devil on every hand. Soldiers full of the Holy Ghost power, and will never give in until Peterborough is won for the King. Capt. Willis"[89]

In the fall of 1886 General William Booth made his first tour of North America. Ten of Canada's most important cities were visited.[90] That this tour included Peterborough, attests to the fact that the Corps was experiencing phenomenal growth.

> Our entry here [Peterborough] created much excitement. Crowds of people had congregated at the railway station to welcome the General! The Staff Brass Band and some 200 Soldiers rapidly formed into procession with torches blazing and hearts burning with expectancy.
>
> On marches the column followed by the war chariot containing the General, Colonel and Commissioner. The streets were lined on either side by crowds of people, and as the band diffused its volumes of rapturous melody upon the gentle evening breezes, it gave our march every appearance of a military procession.
>
> The large Opera House, a building handsomely adapted for the occasion, was comfortably filled by about 2,500 persons. Facing the audience is a large platform full of Officers and Soldiers.
>
> In comes the General amidst the thundering volleys and trumpet blasts of the joyous soldiery. The General rose to speak. His address lasted for about an hour and a quarter. He said that the Salvation

---

[88] Canadian *War Cry*. July 4, 1885.
[89] Canadian *War Cry*. Aug. 8, 1885.
[90] Sandall. Vol. IV. p. 143.

> Army had made an honest attempt to save the dying masses of sinful humanity, and claimed that even if it had been a failure it ought to command the sympathy of the Christian world because it was an honest attempt, but the S. A, has not failed, said he, 'It has been a glorious success.' We feel sure that many a prejudiced and biased mind was led into the light and they learned what the Salvation Army really is. The Peterborough Corps is advancing. About 60 Soldiers are there as living witnesses for Christ.[91]

This was a time when the whole community was aware of The Salvation Army. This may have been the first glimpse of the "Army" for the Payton family. The corps was dramatically influenced by the General's visit. The *War Cry* reported growth both in numbers and spirit. The Commissioner visited Peterborough two months later.

> The Commissioner talked on the 'wonder of the age' and four young men came to our wonderful Saviour, and have been marching and praising God ever since. On Wednesday we had a good time, swore in 15 new soldiers. We had 4 more souls on Thursday, and on Friday 4 more. Grand holiness meeting, a melting and mellowing time, six more out for purity. Big march in the afternoon, 72 being in the ranks.[92]

The corps was a marching and an open-air corps. Many marches were recorded in the *War Cry* and the ranks numbered between sixty and one hundred. It is interesting to note that our tradition of marching and open-airs came from the Methodist Church.

> Capt. Pople; Meetings have been times of power and blessing. Sunday morning several were out seeking deliverance from idols that so hindered their growth in grace, and all professed to receive cleansing through the blood. Afternoon was best, Christians testifying all over the building and telling of the good old times when the Methodists used to march, speak and pray in the open-air, similar to the Army proceedings now.[93]

---

[91] Canadian *War Cry*. Nov. 6, 1886.
[92] Canadian *War Cry*. Jan. 26, 1887.
[93] Canadian War Cry. Feb. 5, 1887.

With time the use of brass bands in Salvation Army ministry became synonymous with our name; however, the first record of the use of a brass instrument in The Christian Mission (one of the early names of The Salvation Army) was in Stockton, England, in 1877. Early efforts were primitive as illustrated from the following *War Cry* report:

> Among the converts are two members of a brass band—one plays a cornet, and to utilize him at once Brother Russell put him with his cornet in the front rank of the procession from South Stockton. He certainly improved the singing and brought crowds along the line of march, wondering curiously what we should do next.[94]

Brass banding was not a part of worship until after the name was changed to The Salvation Army in 1878. In that same year, The Salvation Army was experiencing strong opposition in their open air services in the city of Salisbury, England. A family of musicians, Mr. Fry and his three boys, offered to stand with the Salvationists in support of the street service. They brought along their instruments and accompanied the singing. This innovation caught on quickly, and soon bands were appearing all over England.[95]

The first step towards bringing a band together was to find a drummer. The cadence for marching was set by the drum. All that was needed to march were soldiers and a drum.

The corps was about to celebrate their second year anniversary, and they were already experiencing growth pains. It became obvious they would soon need a larger barracks, and there were already plans in the works to meet that challenge. A grand banquet was planned that included rich and poor, black and white, drunk and sober and everyone seemed to enjoy themselves. A grand march to the railroad station followed where they met Mr. William Gooderham and escorted him to the Opera House for a stirring meeting. His testimony was followed by many others who spoke of the change the Lord had made in their lives. Mr. Cox, an outstanding citizen of the community, gave his testimony and "gave a good donation towards the barracks, $200." Mr. Cox announced:

> Our subscription towards the New Barracks Fund [started at zero] and in a short time the Captain tells me altogether he has about

---

[94] Sandall. Vol. I. p. 211.
[95] Sandall. Vol. II. p. 113.

$1,000 Promised. We are in want of $4,000 more, send it in soon and help [will be] on the way. Amen[96]

Until this time no record was found referring to a Peterborough brass band but there were signs of a beginning on the horizon. An article in the *War Cry* notes that Glory Barker, the drummer, testified "These show times friends, I could never get along without a big drunk and I have often tried to keep sober, but would not. One time I got drunk and got fighting, and the police arrested and put me in the lockup, and some of my old chums busted the door and let me out. But the past is under the blood. Thank God for the Salvation Army."[97] How long Glory Barker was the drummer is not known but the marchers had a cadence.

Salvation Army brass bands were not unknown to Peterborough. The Staff Brass Band was there to welcome William Booth. However there is some question as to whether the community was ready for the first contingency of Peterborough musicians on a November day in 1887. The visiting band led a march to the square, and a group of officers and area soldiers marched as well.

> On Sunday we marched through a strange part of the town, brass band to the front, consisting of cornet, trombone and bombardon [predecessor to the bassoon]. Of course we made a noise and roused up the sinners.[98]

This trio could not yet be called a band. What a humble beginning for a one of Canada's premier bands that in the years to come would grow to have over forty musicians. The growth was instant as the next week's *War Cry* reported:

> In Peterborough the other night some 72 out of 78 were present at roll call and several lay prostrate under the power of God. Things are looking up. Brass Band played on the street for the first time October 30 [1887] and played well.[99]

---

[96] Canadian *War Cry*. May 7, 1887.
[97] Canadian *War Cry*. Oct. 29, 1887.
[98] Canadian *War Cry*. Nov. 12, 1887.
[99] Canadian *War Cry*. Nov. 19, 1887.

It did not take long for opposition to show up. The next month the soldiers were marching to the open-air service sixty-seven strong with the band out front. Some "volunteer boys" blew their bugles to break down our procession, but got left and we were the victors.[100]

In spite of the hindrances, the corps outgrew the capacity of their building. Because it became necessary to turn away so many people from the hall, they decided to "take over" the Opera House.[101]

Three important celebrations took place during the summer of 1888. The cornerstone of the new barracks was laid in a ceremony after a march led by the band as well as a multitude of officers and soldiers from many nearby Army Centers. The seating capacity was estimated to be one thousand with a platform to accommodate two hundred additional people.[102] The second celebration was "A Great Hallelujah Excursion and Picnic at Jubilee Point Monday, July 2nd Dominion Day."[103]

The climax of the special occasions was the dedication of "The new Salvation Army Barracks on Simcoe Street." The front page of the August 11, 1888, edition of the *War Cry* and four additional columns described the three days of services and special events. Each of the incoming trains brought officers and soldiers from Toronto, Montreal, Ottawa and Quebec. It was another time when all of Peterborough was aware of The Salvation Army.

Mysteriously, over time, the band was no longer mentioned in the many reports recorded in the *War Cry*. No explanation was ever found except a short note which appeared in the *War Cry* some years later.

> I heard that nine new recruits were enrolled the other evening at Peterborough, and that the brass band has been brought to life again. It starts its new career with about eleven members and it is hoped that it will not again come to an untimely end. They are under the instruction of a **practical musician**.[104]

---

[100] Canadian *War Cry*. Dec. 10, 1887.
[101] Canadian *War Cry*. Jan. 21, 1888.
[102] Canadian *War Cry*. June 9, 1888.
[103] Canadian *War Cry*. June 23, 1888.
[104] Canadian *War Cry*. Feb. 2, 1890.

BANDMASTER PAYTON AND CHILD,
Peterboro, Ont.

Canadian *War Cry*. August 1, 1896. p.10. Courtesy. The John E. T. Milsaps Collection. Houston Metropolitan Research Center. Houston Public Library. Houston, Texas. With permission The Salvation Army Archives, Canada and Bermuda Territory.

One Payton was already playing cornet in another corps in 1889, and it is believed that the **"practical musician"** mentioned in the February 2, 1890, *War Cry* was William Henry Payton. Current members of the Peterborough Band named William as their first bandmaster and the earliest photographs in the corps band room list him as bandmaster for several decades. He was from a musical family; two of his brothers played in Salvation Army bands, and Edwin and George eventually became Salvation Army officers and played in the St. Thomas Corps Band. George eventually established a blacksmith business in St Thomas, Ontario. We have often wondered how he was able to get his "large and sinewy hands" around a little cornet.

William led a band that was growing in numbers and proficiency. There were almost weekly reports in the *War Cry* of band activity and advancement. Peterborough was gaining the reputation of a Corps on fire for the Lord. While Commissioner Evangeline Booth was visiting she said, "I have heard many good things about Peterborough people from different parties, so I have learned to love you before I had the pleasure of seeing you. Now I have had the pleasure of seeing you, I cannot help loving you more. I am glad that the band boys know how to **Pray as Well as Play**."[105]

Canadian *War Cry*. March 2, 1895. p. 5. Courtesy. The John E. T. Milsaps Collection, Houston Metropolitan Research Center. Houston Public Library. Houston, Texas. With permission The Salvation Army Archives, Canada and Bermuda Territory.

---

[105] Canadian *War Cry*. Sept. 19, 1896.

The members of the Corps were encouragers as indicated in the November 14, 1896, *War Cry*. "The service at Picton was reinforced by Bandmaster Payton and Brother Edmunson of Peterborough." Some of the churches in town were interested in the open air ministry. When the Sunday Schools of the city united for a great celebration in the Court House Park the Senior Brass Band led the music for the demonstration." Rev. J. G. Potter spoke favorably of our open air work and thought the Church of the future would do more in the open air meetings. He thought it would be a good idea to help the Army open-airs, and so gain experience and get their throats more used to the work.[106] After many decades of leading the band, William continued playing under the leadership of successive bandmasters and taught young people to play brass instruments until late in his life.

The corps had a banner year in 1898. General Booth made his second visit to the Peterborough Corps in January, and his daughter Commissioner Evangeline Booth came to town for a three-day campaign in July. It was announced that she would give her "Miss Booth in Rags" message in the last service. She spoke of her slum experience dressed in the garments she wore in the slums. The *War Cry* lauded the work of the corps in the following quotation.

> The juniors of this corps are in splendid shape. They have now seventeen companies [Sunday School Classes]. J.S.S.M. [Junior Soldiers Sergeant Major] Braund's face is all smiles, and it has good reason to be with the great success they are having. I am quite sure in stating that Peterborough has one of the best, if not THE best, J.S. [Junior Soldier] system in North America.[107]

The date of May 29, 1914, is one that remains on the minds of Canadian Salvationists. On that day there occurred the worst tragedy in all their history. The Ocean liner, "Empress of Ireland," carrying some 1,102 passengers of whom 170 were Salvationists, sank within fourteen minutes after being struck by another ship. Because of very heavy fog, a coal carrying cargo ship, the "Storstad," rammed the "Empress of Ireland" precisely in the middle, piercing a huge hole in its side in the area of the boiler room. The Captain of the ship called for full speed ahead to make a run for the shore but with the sudden loss of all power, this was not possible. The ship listed so quickly that only a few of the life boats on one side could be launched. The Salvationists, including the Territorial Commander and his wife, Commissioner and Mrs.

---

[106] Canadian *War Cry*. July 24, 1897.
[107] Canadian *War Cry*. Apr. 22, 1899.

David Rees, the Chief Secretary and his wife, Colonel and Mrs. Sidney Maidment, other officers of Territorial Headquarters and the Canadian Staff Band were among those on their way to an International Congress in England. Of the 170 Salvationists, 130 were lost including the two top leaders and their wives plus all but seven members of the Staff Band.

On the day following the disaster, the Peterborough Corps Band including two members of the Payton family, William and Herbert, went to Montreal by train where they would board the ocean liner, Alaunia, to sail to England and participate in the Congress. William, former bandmaster presently playing baritone, and his sixteen year-old son, Herbert, a cornet player, were oblivious to the disaster in the outgoing sea lanes of the St. Lawrence River. They had chosen to travel on this ship as it was ten dollars cheaper than the "Empress." When they arrived, they learned about the terrible accident. There was some thought of not proceeding, but they reconsidered and continued with their travel plans. Since they were the only other band from Canada scheduled to participate in the Congress, it became their responsibility to fill some of the Staff Band's engagements. The Canadian *War Cry* of the time recorded the band's participation.[108]

We began this chapter with the title of *A New Life in the New World*. As we review the chapter, a deeper meaning unfolds. When the Payton family met The Salvation Army, a new SPIRITUAL life was born that has continued for generations.

Left to right—Ethel, Herbert, Beulah, William, Sarah and Pearl Payton.

---

[108] Canadian *War Cry*. July 18, 1914.

Chapter Nine

New Horizons

"Jabez cried out to the God of Israel, Oh, that you would bless me and enlarge my territory! Let your hand be with me".
I Chronicles 4:10 NIV

Since we know the approximate date when Margaret farewelled from the corps in Leek, we can assume that she was part of the following upheaval of officers. According to the London *War Cry* issues of May 4 and May 11, 1889, seven hundred fifty officers received communications called "change of stations."

The Territorial Commander of Canada occasionally issued an invitation to people in Great Britain via the London *War Cry* to emmigrate to Canada. This inferred that the Army leadership would assist them in finding employment. Because family lore tells us that since Margaret was being transferred to the United States, her stepfather and mother were probably aware of the offer in the *War Cry* and decided to cross the Atlantic and settle in Canada in order to be nearer to her. She decided to travel with them and to proceed from there to her appointment.

While there she attended the seventh anniversary of the establishment of The Salvation Army in Canada which was also the farewell of Commissioner and Mrs. Coombs from the Canadian Command. This was celebrated from September 14 through 19, 1889. There were at least two people who knew Margaret attended this activity. One was Major John Margetts who was stationed in the Merthyr Tydfil Corps shortly before her, and the other was the Territorial Commander, Commissioner Thomas Coombs. He had been her first divisional commander when she was stationed in the South Wales Division. How she met the Commissioner at this time is not known. Major Margetts might have recognized her and introduced her to the Commissioner or she might have just been identified from the platform. According to what Margaret used to say, the Commissioner asked her what she was doing in Canada and her response was, "I am under orders to an appointment in the United States and have traveled with my parents who are immigrating here. I will be going there shortly." He asked her if she would prefer to remain in Canada to which she responded in a positive manner. He said, "I will arrange it."

An interesting sidelight to this conversation is the fact that The Salvation Army in Canada was then experiencing what some might call "growing pains." At least one officer was not happy with the leadership and its administrative style. He accused them of not allowing Canadians to progress to leadership positions, reserving this for officers imported from England. He published a pamphlet with all of his accusations and was able to influence about one hundred officers to resign including one who was in an administrative position.[109] Thus Margaret arrived at a particular time when there was a shortage of officers. The family often wondered how the Commissioner was able to convince International Headquarters to allow her to remain in Canada. This need probably is the rationale he used to convince them. Regardless of the reason, she didn't reach the United States at that time.

Strathroy, Ontario.

According to Margaret, Strathroy, Ontario, was her first appointment in Canada.[110] For a considerable time, we were not able to confirm this through reviewing issues of the *War Cry* or the listing of officers stationed at this appointment from July 4, 1889. Fortunately, through the diligence of the Salvation Army Heritage Center in Canada, this was finally verified. She was there only a scant two weeks.[111]

---

[109] Moyles, Robert Gordon. *The Blood and Fire in Canada*. Edmonton, Canada. AGM Publications. 2004. p. 113
[110] Canadian *War Cry*. Jan. 5, 1929.
[111] Canadian *War Cry*. Jan. 5, 1929.

Ingersoll, Ontario

Margaret arrived at her next appointment, the Ingersoll Corps, on July 18, 1889. Once again we had difficulty authenticating Margaret's claim through the listing of officers stationed there, however, recent information confirmed it. In addition there was found in the weekly reports of the sale of the *War Cry* that she was there until January 30, 1890. The Divisional Officer, Major Baugh, visited the corps for a grand celebration on December 21 to officially commission the Ingersoll band. The band from Woodstock, Ontario, also participated in the celebration.

Margaret used to share with her children the story about one soldier in Ingersoll who was a hard worker but only if she considered the task at hand to be an important one. The soldier, Minnie Peart, married a widower considerably older than she and had one daughter, Aimee, who also married young. Her daughter Aimee Semple McPherson became famous for founding the "Foursquare Gospel Church" and for a questionable disappearance some years later in California. She and another individual were charged with conspiracy, but the court eventually dismissed the case.[112]

In May 1890, Margaret was invited back to the corps to be the special guest for a Sunday. She spoke on the love of God which, according to the *War Cry*, "made the sinners feel their lost condition, and one person accepted the Lord."[113]

St. Thomas, Ontario

The St. Thomas Corps was one of the earliest corps to be opened in Canada. Margaret's appointment to this corps was destined to have an enormous influence on her.

After officially opening the work in the United States, Commissioner George Scott Railton was in Canada for a short period. It is known that he held some open-air meetings in Halifax in 1881. Additionally a few Salvationist immigrants conducted unofficial Army meetings in Toronto in the same year. However, the generally recognized date of the commencement of The Salvation Army in Canada is 1882. Jack Addie and Joe Ludgate, former Salvationists from England, held their first meetings in May 1882 in

---

[112] Creighton, David. *Losing the Empress*. Toronto: Dundurn Press. 2000. p. 99.
[113] London *War Cry*. May 17, 1890.

London, Ontario. Nearby, the St. Thomas Corps was officially opened on February 3, 1883. Similar to what happened in other new openings, the corps grew rapidly and quickly and became a functioning ministry.

Margaret arrived in St. Thomas on January 30, 1890. For a period of at least seven weeks, the name Bach is listed both in St. Thomas and in Paris, Ontario. This mystery was resolved when we learned that her brother Richard William Bach had been reaccepted as an officer in the United States in January of 1889. He was transferred to Canada in January of 1890. He eventually held three appointments in Canada: Paris, Collingwood and Midland.

Margaret's appointment to St. Thomas took place at a very critical time. Her son Edwin recorded the circumstances in the following manner, "One time her Divisional Commander, Brigadier Philpot, wanted her to go with him to the St. Thomas Corps for a meeting . . . . When they left the meeting, the Brigadier asked my mother what she thought of that. She said, "That's a real hot spot." He replied, "That's your next appointment."[114]

The reference to St. Thomas being "a real hot spot" undoubtedly refers to a split in the corps. Some of the band had resigned over a controversy with headquarters. I quote from the book, *The Streets, Our Cathedral* by Ted Palmer, the history of the St. Thomas Corps:

> On January 6, 1890, the *Times* reported simply that Lieut. Howard of the Salvation Army farewelled at the barracks yesterday. Such news items appeared every six months or so in those early years of the Army and, therefore, was not given any particular emphasis or elaboration.
>
> However, the farewell of Capt. Gilroy and Lieut. Howard was not a routine change in leadership as further articles and letters to the editor over the next two months would make clear. The story that unfolded was of a most unfortunate sequence of events that threatened to fatally damage the great and Godly work of the previous seven years.
>
> Capt. Gilroy and Lieut. Howard arrived in St. Thomas in June 1889. Both ladies were attractive, well-educated and competent both as singers and public speakers. Capt. Gilroy tended to be

---

[114] Payton, Edwin. Personal recorded interview. 1983.

rather blunt when conveying the truth, and both ladies were somewhat independent by nature.

When they arrived at the St. Thomas quarters, they were shocked. Great chunks of plaster were off the wall, the floors coated with layers of filth, and the beds alive with vermin. At their Welcome meeting that night, Capt. Gilroy shared her dismay with the comrades of the corps, offering a personal tour of the disaster area to anyone who doubted her word. Some of the comrades immediately took up a collection to get some new linen for the ladies to sleep on.

Over the next weeks, further donations were obtained. One of the largest amounts came from a special concert the band put on to raise funds to improve the quarters. All money was used for direct purchases for quarters furnishings, the two officers selecting and paying for items as the money came in. The amounts involved were listed in the corps cash book as "Donations for Furnishings."

However, not all the soldiers were keen on enhancing the physical comforts of their officers. One wrote to the Territorial Commissioner complaining about such use of funds.

Soon a disciplinary letter was sent from headquarters. Gilroy and Howard, the letter asserted, were guilty of improper handling of Salvation Army funds as they had not sent to Divisional Headquarters the ten percent of income that was rightly theirs. The officers were to forward that tithe immediately.

A day later, the Bandmaster also received a reprimand. The band had acted wrongly in using its instruments and talents for this sort of fund raising. It was told that it should assist in making up out of its members' pockets the missing tenth.

The officers were so disheartened by what they considered an attack on their integrity that they resigned. The bandsmen were so incensed by the reprimand and demand, that they went on strike. The newspaper, covering such bad news with peculiar thoroughness, dropped its guise of objectivity and began referring to headquarters as "the Chief Moguls."

The controversy flamed for nearly three months. For some weeks, the corps was unofficered. Apparently Gilroy and Howard stayed on in the community. Gilroy married a financially comfortable local bachelor; Miss Howard appears as a singer in subsequent musical nights at the Corps.

Finally, Cadet Massecar was freed from her responsibilities in Woodstock to oversee St. Thomas **until a more experienced officer could be sent.** The second week in February the Bandmaster was informed that unless he and his bandsmen returned to the Army and their duties there at once, they were to turn their instruments over to the new commanding officers.

A significant turning point came soon after that when the paper reported that "The Salvation Army band is about to re-organize."

By March 23, the band was back in the streets playing its rousing music in the open airs. Outcome of the battle: Satan defeated.[115]

It was into this "real hot spot" situation that Margaret, "**a more experienced officer,**" found her name on the official listing of appointments for the St. Thomas Corps records: "Capt. Bach; Ltd. [Lieutenant] Osmond; and Cadet Weston." Fortunately it appears that one of the bandsmen who did not abandon the corps was George Charles Payton who became prominent in the family history.

---

[115] Palmer, Ted. *The Streets, Our Cathedral.* St. Thomas: Privately published. 1982. p. 24-26.

Captain Margaret Bach standing, Lieutenant Osmond and Cadet Weston.

According to research Margaret continued in that appointment until the end of August that year. There was one *War Cry* report which is important to quote:

> We can still report victory here. We are having some blessed times in St. Thomas. Souls are getting saved. Since our last report a dear friend who used to attend our meetings HAS GONE TO HEAVEN. She was only saved just in time. We buried her under the flag. Two souls were saved last week and two last night. To God be all the glory! Our baby band is coming on fine. All around the prospects look brighter. Maggie Bach, Capt.[116]

Gravenhurst

Margaret arrived at this appointment on June 12, 1890. We have no information of her time there, but it is interesting to note that her son Edwin was stationed as the assistant in this corps some thirty-five years later. This was his first appointment following his period of training. In the intervening years something happened here which merits sharing. One officer had been

---

[116] Canadian *War Cry*. Aug. 30, 1890.

disloyal and unchristian and had left a large debt so the city council had requested that The Salvation Army close the corps. There was one faithful soldier, "Granny" Stickles, who insured that all of the indebtedness would be repaid. Every Saturday she would display the Army flag she had kept and give her testimony on the main street. She was so respected by the people in the town that eventually the same city council requested that The Salvation Army return. When Edwin was appointed to Gravenhurst, "Granny" was still there. She was the first woman Salvationist to receive "The Order of the Founder,"[117] the highest award that The Salvation Army confers. Margaret was there only two months.

Lisgar Street

Once again following the practice of the day, after a short stay in Gravenhurst, Margaret was appointed on August 8, 1890, to the Toronto No. 3 Corps which was also called the Lisgar Street Corps. There is some discrepancy between the official date of her appointment and the reports of *War Cry* sales in the weekly publication. It was the practice at different times to publish the number of sales of the *War Cry* in the weekly editions. Undoubtedly this was done trying to encourage others to imitate the success of those who were doing well. With the exception of Strathroy, the Bach name appeared each week under the name of the corps where Margaret was stationed, along with the amount sold. With this information available, we were able to track her movements from corps to corps.

The Lisgar Street Corps was one of the outstanding corps in Canada. Sometime after she farewelled from there, it was made one of the training garrison corps. Little is known of her time there with the exception of a few articles that appeared in various *War Cry* editions.

> FROM LISGAR STREET
> Major Spooner and I spent a very enjoyable day at [the] Lisgar Street barracks on Sunday. God displayed His power in saving and sanctifying. Three came for sanctification at the holiness meeting. One of them was a sister who disobeyed the call of God, and would not go into the field. They all got the blessing. Hallelujah. I was sorry to find some who acknowledged they were not right with God and refused to get right. I pray that God will open their eyes. Anyone who is wrong and won't get right, is nothing more or

---

[117] Payton, Edwin. Personal recorded interview. 1983.

less than a sinner. We had a grand time in Bellwood's Park. When we arrived we found the Arthur Street Corps commanded by Adjt. [Adjutant] Leonard when the united Corps went in with all their heart.

You should have heard a sister talk on pride. While she spoke some of the people were seen to drop their heads and hit the ground with their parasol. The crowd was very large and a good collection was taken up.

At night in Lisgar Street barracks we had six precious souls crying for mercy. The tears flowed freely, and there were some genuine convictions. [118]

Under a column "Tidbits by the Junior Soldier Warrior,"

LISGAR STREET—Was my next meeting. After being with the children I took the holiness meeting. God came upon us and many a soul went away strengthened and refreshed. We had a good crowd and a heavenly time. Staff Captain Bennett.[119]

The last reference to her time in Lisgar Street was the following announcement:

"GREAT RESCUE DEMONSTRATION at Lisgar Street, Toronto III on Monday, November 17, with the visit of Mrs. Commissioner Adams leading."[120]

Due to health concerns, it was necessary for Margaret to take a sick furlough on January 29, 1891, from the Lisgar Street Corps. As it turned out, this was to be her last appointment as a single officer. While stationed in St. Thomas, she had become acquainted with one member of the Payton family. She was to become a part of it.

---

[118] Canadian *War Cry*. Sept. 27, 1890.
[119] Canadian *War Cry*. Nov. 1, 1890.
[120] Canadian *War Cry*. Nov. 15, 1890.

Chapter Ten

Finding Her Love

"Many, O Lord my God, are the wonders you have done."
Psalm 40:5 NIV

The reason the Bach/Goodchild family finally moved to St. Thomas could not be confirmed, but evidence shows that this is where they eventually settled. The most reasonable explanation is that they moved there when Margaret was appointed the Salvation Army officer in that city. Margaret had, once again, taken a sick furlough following what had been a vigorous time in the Lisgar Street Corps. On several occasions, according to her own words, she needed a time of rest to reestablish her health. It is clear that this happened with many officers of the day. The demanding schedule they were required to keep exhausted them. It is also important to remember that medical research was not as advanced as we now know it, and there was no other recourse but to stop for awhile and recuperate. Another requisite that the officers had to contend with was the frequency of their transfers to new appointments. In a recent publication, some observations were made for the cause of the frequent moves.

> This frequent change in the tenure of the field officer [was] a deliberate policy adopted by the Army for definite reasons. The most cogent reason for this practice is the desire to give the corps the impetus which comes from new spiritual guidance. Most of the field officers have had little theological training and as officers have little time or money to continue their studies, therefore, after

a period many of them are, as one officer put it, "preached out" and a new officer brings a new inspirational message to the Corps.[121]

This also was the cause of many officers leaving the work as their families were not able to adjust. An interesting sidelight to this problem is found in papers preserved by the Richard William Bach family. It is a letter written by Ballington Booth (his training home principal in London) in response to a letter written by Richard. In light of later actions by Ballington, who resigned his officership, it is a document important to share.

> CONGRESS HALL
> LOWER Clapton,
> London, E
> 18th Nov. 1883
> My dear Bach,
>
> I have received your letter of some days back and I am sorry that you should have been moved so much from one Station to another, though you will at last settle & be happy in Camelford.
>
> I am thankful the Lord is so near and good to your soul
>
> I have not much fear of those we send from the Home succeeding if they will but allow God to be <u>all in all to their souls</u>. It is when self pride & worldly mindedness creep in that they begin to grow lukewarm and indifferent, and fail.
>
> May God keep you red hot in His love and zeal for the sake of His Son.
>
> Test yourself night & morning, asking yourself how much you have gained of Him, of His nature, of His love.
>
> God bless you
> Yours affectly in Him
> **The Salvation Army**
> **Ballington Booth**
> Lieut. Bach
> Camelford[122]

Richard eventually joined the family in St. Thomas as we will see through several *War Cry* reports.

---

[121] *Eastern Territorial Historical Society Bulletin.* June 2011.
[122] Papers from Richard William Bach preserved by the family.

Margaret began her sick furlough sometime near the end of January 29, 1891, and she and George Charles Payton were married on May 25, 1891.

George Charles and Margaret Elizabeth Payton.

George continued to be a bandsman in the corps. Banding had been of interest to the Payton family as illustrated by the commitment of his brother William in the Peterborough Corps. Another evidence of George´s enthusiasm for banding is a photograph that has been held in the family for over a century. The newly formed Household Troops Band from England was invited to tour the Canadian Territory from October 1887 to February 1888 that included a visit to St. Thomas. Besides exposing the Army to the public and sharing the Gospel message, one of the purposes of the tour was to raise one thousand pounds to complete a rescue home, and they also raised money for the "Sick and Wounded Fund" for officers. Undoubtedly one of their sources of income was the sale of copies of a photograph of the band which apparently George treasured over the years.[123]

---

[123] *Theme Online*. Newsletter. Apr. 10, 2008.

Margaret continued to be active in the St. Thomas Corps as a local officer, namely Junior Soldier Sergeant Major. We found this through an article written in the *War Cry* by her brother, Richard William. This tells us that he also was no longer an officer but was the Special Correspondent to the *War Cry* for the St. Thomas Corps.[124] One of his reports concludes with the following:

> Last Sunday, we had a novel experience. While on the march, we were caught in a blizzard, which came upon us so heavily that the band had to stop playing. You should have seen us marching single file, snow nearly knee deep. It was real good.[125]

Richard William, Jane and son Fred Bach.

A later report tells us that Sergeant Bach was selling the *War Cry*. Finally we learn from the *War Cry* the following:

---

[124] Canadian *War Cry*. Apr. 29, 1893.
[125] Canadian *War Cry*. Mar. 25, 1893.

Brother and Sister Payton have farewelled. We shall miss them as Sister Payton was the J. S. S. M. and Brother Payton was a bandsman: but our loss will be Dutton's gain, as they have gone near there; as they will be about six miles from a corps they would not be able to get to meetings very often, but they intend to stick to their uniform and be S. A. soldiers.[126]

For several years, the byline R. W. Bach appeared at the end of the articles in the *War Cry* from St. Thomas, but a new name, Bandsman Goodchild, appeared in March 1895. Robert Charles Goodchild was a step brother of Margaret and Richard. Gradually we saw more evidence of participation on the part of the family in the corps activities. Robert became the bandmaster and contributed new songs to the *War Cry* which was the custom at that time. Mrs. Goodchild wrote a song also, but it is not clear whether she was Robert's wife or mother. Perhaps the most interesting discovery is the fact that Mother Goodchild of St. Thomas sold the *War Cry*. It is more apt that this person was the mother of Richard and Margaret because she was recorded in the *War Cry* as doing this for several years. But we are getting ahead of our story. We need to return to 1892.

George and Margaret's family began to grow. On April 5, 1892, George Ernest was born and on January 16, 1895, Louisa Mary followed. By this time they were living in Dutton, Ontario, and undoubtedly George had established his blacksmith shop. Little is known of their time in that town, but two important events took place in St. Thomas which, undoubtedly, they attended.

On August 13, 1894, Herbert Booth, Commander of Canadian forces and son of the Founder, visited the corps for a special meeting. This was to be overshadowed by the visit of General William Booth on January 29, 1895.[127] Every effort was made to make this an outstanding event in the city. The local authorities, the mayor and a leading judge, chaired the meeting. The principal of the Alma College gave the welcoming address and another judge hosted him while in the city. The opera house was rented for this special occasion.

The *St. Thomas Times* recorded the event calling Booth "a remarkable man" and the Salvation Army "a great movement," and the reporter wrote that Booth "received an enthusiastic welcome from the citizens of St. Thomas." It

---

[126] Canadian *War Cry*. Apr. 29, 1893.
[127] Canadian *War Cry*. Jan. 19, 1895.

described General Booth as a "man of intense enthusiasm and earnestness." Physically, it sketched The Salvation Army Founder as a tall man of venerable appearance. It further states that Booth "speaks with great rapidity, keeping his hands behind his back, but gesticulates when he becomes more animated, though not very gracefully."[128]

With so many of the family living in St. Thomas, most assuredly George, Margaret, George Ernest, and Louisa found a place to stay and were present on this important occasion. The visit of the Founder was likely to have had a profound impact on them. Remember that Margaret was commissioned by him in Exeter Hall in London and that he then made mention of her and her brother Richard William.

At the time of General Booth's visit, George and Margaret made the decision to reenter the ministry; perhaps they were so inspired by the Founder's message and by the moving of the Holy Spirit in their hearts. It is also possible that the Founder personally encouraged them to do so.

Another intriguing aspect is the fact that Margaret had been stationed in Brynmawr and Merthyr-Tydfil, just a few miles from where the then Captain John Edward Margetts was serving. Major Margetts, then the Divisional Commander, may have been endeavoring to convince them to become officers. Could he have taken advantage of the visit of the Founder and brought them together? In any case, just four months after this, they were accepted as Cadet Captains and some months later accepted their first appointment. There appears to be some confusion which has been impossible for us to untangle so we will just share the information that we have and let you decide.

George and Margaret were accepted as Cadet Captains on May 21, 1895, but they didn't go to their first appointment until September 19. There must have been some sort of training during this period. They may not have required Margaret to have the training as she had already been a cadet and an officer in England and Canada. In addition, Louisa Mary was born in January of that year, and Margaret may have been allowed to remain at home during the early months of the baby's development while George completed his training.

---

[128] Palmer, Ted. *The Streets our Cathedral.* St. Thomas Corps. Privately published. 1982. p.33.

According to a *War Cry* report written by Robert Goodchild, "Cadet Payton farewelled for the work" from St. Thomas.[129] George's brother Edwin became an officer at about this same time. He had moved to St. Thomas and was active as a bandsman there. The next observation is that the reference in the report is singular, i.e., Cadet Payton. In any case, there was a Cadet Payton who received a very special training, unique to say in the least. A photograph of the crew of the yacht "William Booth" appeared on the front page of the *War Cry*. One of the crew members, holding a valve trombone, is identified as Cadet Payton.[130] Is it George or is it Edwin? The mystery remains.

In 1844, a fifteen-year old William Booth made his often quoted promise that "God should have all there is of William Booth."[131] That decision had a much greater impact on the world than he could have imagined in his wildest dreams. At the fiftieth anniversary of that event, there was a jubilee celebration around the world.[132] In Canada, Commandant Herbert Booth, the commander of the Canadian forces, decided to celebrate it by establishing fifty faith-challenging projects. They included a Territorial Congress, an increase of three hundred new officers, five thousand new junior soldiers, thirteen new corps buildings, seventeen social institutions, the renovation of several buildings, a special *War Cry* issue and a number of other specific projects, in particular, "A Salvation Navy." This was to include a schooner for Newfoundland, a steamboat for the lakes and a steam launch for British Columbia. This is where the Payton family enters the story.

On the 31st of July in 1894 with great fanfare, the yacht "William Booth" was dedicated by Commandant Herbert Booth. It was seventy-two feet long, could sleep sixteen persons and carry one hundred twenty passengers. During that first summer, the vessel traveled about conducting evangelistic meetings in different ports of call. One of the goals that year was to receive and transport William Booth who was to visit in the fall.[133] Unfortunately fire destroyed some of the superstructure of the vessel which took it out of commission for several weeks.[134] It was reported back in service prior to the arrival of the Founder. While transporting him to Gananoque, the crew

---

[129] Canadian *War Cry*. March 2, 1895.
[130] Canadian *War Cry*. July 20, 1895.
[131] Sandall, Vol. I. p. 4.
[132] Canadian *War Cry*. May 19, 1894.
[133] Canadian *War Cry*. July 21, 1894—Aug. 18, 1894.
[134] Canadian *War Cry*. Sept. 1, 1894.

realized that the ship was losing power. A leak in the boiler forced them to use the service of a tug to pull them safely to their destination where there was an enthusiastic crowd awaiting him.[135]

In the spring of 1895, there were announcements in the *War Cry* encouraging young men to apply for crew positions during the summer's evangelistic campaigns. Eventually a crew of twenty was established which included a brass band of twelve. This is when the previously mentioned photo appears which includes Cadet Payton.

---

[135] Canadian War Cry. Nov. 10, 1894.

OUR SALVATION MARINERS.

The Crew of the "William Booth" now Touring the Great Lakes on Salvation Service.

The Crew of the William Booth. Canadian War Cry, July 20, 1895. Courtesy of the John E. T. Milsaps collection, Houston Metropolitan Research Center, Houston Public Library. Houston, Texas. With permission The Salvation Army Archives, Canada and Bermuda Territory.

The Yacht, William Booth.
Artist—Mark Payton

Both the Canadian and the American *War Cry* include prolific accounts of their successful evangelistic endeavors on each side of the border. The original evangelistic purpose of the acquisition of the vessel was being fulfilled. Two accounts from the American *War Cry* illustrate this.

> The Canadian yacht had been at No. 2 (Cleveland, Ohio) on Saturday night, and they were also with the brigadier at the same place Sunday morning. After an excellent march, we had a splendid crowd inside, a holiness and salvation meeting together. In the Saturday p. m. and Sunday monthly meeting the yacht got $21.00. The brigadier gave us an excellent powerful address on Levi, the publican, who 'left all, rose up, and followed Christ.'
>
> The Canadian yacht is visiting Toledo, Sandusky, Elyria, Cleveland and Ashtabula. We bespeak for our comrades a warm welcome at

these places. We pray that they may be the means of winning many souls for God and building up the work of the Army in general. We believe they will. God bless them, and their labors among us. Reports to hand are that they had twelve souls in Toledo, their first Sunday.[136]

Serving as crew members on the yacht was a very special and unusual type of training for officership but effective in the practical sense. It is likely that classes were held during the periods of travel between the ports of call. Before we leave the story of the yacht "William Booth," we will relate the following event. Commissioner Evangeline Booth was scheduled to arrive in June 1896 to take command of the Canadian Territory following her brother and sister-in-law Commandant Herbert and Cornelie Booth. To commemorate this important event, a very colorful arrival ceremony was arranged featuring the ship.

---

[136] New York *War Cry*. Aug. 10, 1895

Chapter Eleven

Reengagement in the Battle

"My zeal wears me out, for my enemies ignore your words."
Psalm 119:139 NIV

AMHERSTBURG, ONTARIO

. . . Mrs. Cadet-Captain Payton, speaking for herself and her husband, 'we mean to be faithful and true to the old flag. We mean to go for sinners, and bring them to the dear Saviour, who shed His blood for them. I am, doing my best to help; though I cannot do all I would with my two little children, but God will help me to glorify His name I know. God bless you till we meet in the great victory morning.'[137]

With these words Margaret expressed her own feelings and those of her husband George. It is fortunate to have this quote revealed in a column, entitled "From Mrs. Booth's Office Table" that Mrs. Commandant Herbert Booth initiated late in 1895 in the Canadian *War Cry*. Apparently she encouraged women officers to be in direct contact with her; her column consisted of a series of letters to which she sometimes added her comments.

Captain and Mrs. Payton's first appointment following their return to officership was Amherstburg, Ontario. It is a town situated on the Detroit

---

[137] Canadian *War Cry*. Feb. 29, 1896.

River across from the state of Michigan in the United States. According to records they were there from September 19, 1895, until March 12, 1896. Little is known of their time there, but it is interesting to see the signature of Major John Edward Margetts (the officer who was acquainted with Margaret early in her Salvation Army experience in Wales) on their appointment orders.

ESSEX, ONTARIO

The next appointment to Essex, Ontario, began on March 12, 1896, to August 14, 1896. Other than the mention of Mrs. Captain Payton in Essex in the list of *War Cry* sellers, there is no documentation of their ministry there.

BLENHEIM, ONTARIO

Margaret and George arrived in Blenheim, Ontario, on August 14, 1896. The Blenheim Corps was blessed to have an efficient *War Cry* correspondent, and thus there was more information preserved about their ministry during this period. Their first memorable event at the corps was the Harvest Festival celebration. The Western Ontario Division had established a prize for the most outstanding Harvest Festival display that they did not win. The Essex Corps won the one dollar prize, but as a result of that contest, there is an excellent photograph taken concerning Blenheim´s effort. The *War Cry* reported: "Target bursted. To God be all the glory.—Captain Payton."[138]

The Blenheim Corps Harvest Festival display of the fall of 1896.

---

[138] Canadian *War Cry*, Oct. 24, 1896.

This appears to have been their favorite appointment they had together in spite of the fact that they suffered their greatest tragedy while there. Perhaps the reason for this is the support that their soldiers gave them during their very difficult experience.

In the photograph we see George, Margaret, George Ernest, baby Louisa Mary and the soldiers of the corps. This was probably the last photograph of George Ernest since he died of diphtheria on December 8, 1896. George and Margaret were on sick furlough in St. Thomas, Ontario, as she was expecting the birth of their third child, Edwin Victor. Not only did George Ernest die, but Louisa Mary became ill with the same disease.

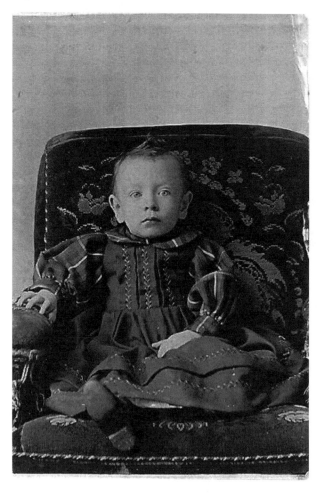

George Ernest Payton.

"A Mother´s hope a father´s joy,
Death´s hand hath her laid low.
God gave and took our darling boy,
To His command we bow."
(Inscription on the tombstone.)

The following report appeared in the War Cry:

> Captain and Mrs. Payton's boy has been called to Glory from Blenheim. Both the Captain and his wife have also been sick.[139] They were quarantined for twenty-one days, and on the last day, Edwin Victor was born. His dedication was reported as follows, 'Sunday afternoon Captain and Mrs. Payton's baby boy was given to God and the Army.'[140]

Margaret was so saddened by this loss that she saved all of the letters of condolence they received. Among those who were part of the outpouring of sympathy were Field Commissioner Evangeline Booth, the family, and the soldiers of the Blenheim Corps as well as other corps. An officer who had been sent to Blenheim to supply leadership during their absence kept the Paytons abreast of all that was happening there. There were those who wondered if they would return to Blenheim. In fact there was a period of a few weeks when there was no officer on duty. The *War Cry* reported that the soldiers carried on the ministry until their return. The heartfelt sympathy expressed by the comrades of the corps most assuredly was the reason that George and Margaret held special places in their hearts for them. As will be seen later, George and Margaret were invited back to Blenheim for some special events.

Whether the following report refers to something that happened while they were in Blenheim or while they were on sick furlough is uncertain. It does indicate an alive and active corps.

> A NARROW ESCAPE—BLENHEIM—One lad, who was very drunk Sunday night and caused some trouble, got saved the next night, also two backsliders. One lady, who should have got right on Sunday, took very ill the following week, and when the end seemed near promised God she would obey, and sent for the Captain, and there and then got saved. Hallelujah! Sinner, don't trifle with the offer of Salvation.—Captain Ottaway for Captain Payton.[141]

Early in 1897 Field Commissioner Evangeline Booth challenged the Salvationists with an outreach campaign called, "The Siege of the Lost." It was more commonly referred to as "The Siege." It was a concentrated

---

[139] Canadian *War Cry*. Jan. 2, 1897.
[140] Canadian *War Cry*. Mar. 13, 1897.
[141] Canadian *War Cry*. Jan. 2, 1897.

evangelistic effort which took place between February 28 and April 28, 1897. The principle purpose was explained in an article by Colonel Jacobs in the *War Cry*.

> The Siege of the Lost to every soldier of the Salvation Army should mean individual effort, the principle of reproduction carried into practice, the duty of one soldier to make another soldier, every possible effort to be made to bring every one of Christ's present followers into active service.[142]

Detailed recommendations appeared weekly in the *War Cry* regarding steps the soldiers should take in this effort. The first period was to be an intense evangelistic effort including extra prayer meetings, extra sales of the *War Cry*, outdoor evangelism as well as indoor zealous preaching. Each week reports appeared, relaying news about the progress that was made. The second month was to be dedicated to the preparation and enrollment of the new converts. In spite of their recent loss, George and Margaret returned in sufficient time to participate in this effort, and there are some reports about this.[143]

> Three days' special meeting, with a Banquet and Jubilee, led by Staff-Captain Turner, of London, and officers from surrounding Corps. At the Half Night-of-Prayer eight came out for Sanctification.—Ina Groom. The Blenheim Officers stamp special announcements on their *War Crys* with a rubber stamp outfit.[144]

> From Captain Payton, Blenheim, comes the news re. The Siege: Had a good start; soldiers all took hold of it beautifully. The first day's fighting wound up with four souls in the fountain. Praise God! We give Him all the glory. You can count on Blenheim. We mean victory. The Provincial Officer and Chancellor have led some wonderful Siege engagements at London, Chatham, Ridgetown, Blenheim, Essex, Windsor, and other places. At the four first mentioned, either 'Three hours at the Cross' or Half-Nights of Prayer were held, in which goodly numbers sought full Salvation, and almost every one pledged themselves to go in for all they were worth to make the Siege a huge success. BLENHEIM. C.O.

---

[142] Canadian *War Cry*. Mar. 6, 1897.
[143] Canadian *War Cry*. Mar. 6, 1897.
[144] Canadian *War Cry*. Mar. 13, 1897.

Captain Payton, 93 *War Crys*. Backsliders are coming home, Great day yesterday, Sunday, enrollment of four recruits, and commissioning Local Officers at night was the crowning time, when four souls volunteered for Salvation, making five for the week. [We] finished with a hallelujah wind up. Ina Groom. Cor.[145]

With permission The Salvation Army Archives, Canada and Bermuda Territory.

---

[145] Canadian *War Cry*. Mar. 20, 1897.

LEAMINGTON, ONTARIO

As was the norm, their time in Blenheim was short and on May 13, 1897, they reported to Leamington, Ontario. There is scant information on their time there except the following *War Cry* reports.

> LEAMINGTON—After a long fight, our Officers, Captain Fell and Lieutenant Ogilvie have gone. Last Saturday and Sunday we welcomed our new Officers, Captain and Mrs. Payton, also Lieutenant Mumford. We had a blessed time of victory. I hear rumors of a Brass and String Band[146].

This demonstrates George's continued interest in brass bands.

> LEAMINGTON—Hot weather not very favorable for our indoor meetings, so we are doing our duty by lifting Christ up to the dying world in the open-air [meetings]. Captain Payton has secured a nice grove in the centre of the town, and this is where you will find us; this is where we are!—E. Rutledge, for Captain Payton[147]

> Leamington Corps has just had a visit from Dr. Logan, the saved Indian. The meetings were well attended, the "Press" reporting very favorably upon them. Crowds on the streets were large. A special afternoon meeting brought in $12.50. Captain Payton is in command of this Corps.[148]

WALLACEBURG, ONTARIO

September 16, 1897, finds George and Margaret in Wallaceburg, and again there is meager information except what has been gleaned from the *War Cry*.

> Wallaceburg, Ont.—We have been having good meetings here. Soldiers all on fire for souls. One soul yielded last night. We expect a great break in the devil's ranks soon. Sister Mrs. Brown lectured at Port Lampton on the League of Mercy and the Rescue work. It was worth hearing. We are all working to smash our target this

---

[146] Canadian *War Cry,* June 12, 1897.
[147] Canadian *War Cry.* Aug. 28, 1897
[148] Canadian *War Cry.* Oct. 2, 1897.

> Self-Denial. [Annual financial effort for the mission field.] Jesus is at the helm. Bless Him.—Sergt. Flossie Smith for Capt. Payton.[149]

We wonder if daughter, Flossie Violet, was named after the corps' correspondent (Flossie Smith) because it was only a matter of months after they moved from Wallaceburg when she was born.

> Wallaceburg,—Splendid meetings all day. One soul out for a hallelujah breakfast. He had wandered away from God. Three backsliders returned to the fold since last report. Sister Brown of the League of Mercy lectured to us on the Social work last Saturday night [and] to a large crowd, many hearts were touched. We smashed our S. D. [Self Denial—missionary collection] target. Hallelujah!—Sergt. F. Smith, for Capt. Payton[150]

> Wallaceburg,—Victory is ours. Four souls. Since last report our officers were in Toronto. Got well blessed. There were many saved at the General [Booth's] meetings, but Jesus did not forget this little corner. We have the faith to reach our Siege target. Much conviction among the sinners.—Sergt. Flossie Smith, for Capt. Payton.[151]

> Wallaceburg.—We are winning. One week of revival at Port Lambton. Two souls for Jesus. God has laid his hand on one of our dear comrades and took him to Himself. His earthly scenes are ended, his life's battles fought and won. Now he is safe in the arms of Jesus. We are going on to do our best for Jesus.—Sergeant Flossie Smith, for Captain Payton.[152]

According to records from March 31, 1898, George and Margaret were once again on sick furlough until May 25, 1898.

---

[149] Canadian *War Cry*. Dec. 18, 1897.
[150] Canadian *War Cry*. Jan. 8, 1898.
[151] Canadian *War Cry*. Mar. 12, 1898.
[152] Canadian *War Cry*. Apr. 2, 1898.

PARIS, ONTARIO

Except for the fact that it can be confirmed through records that George and Margaret were stationed in Paris from May 25, 1898, until June 14, 1898, there is no additional information regarding their time there. Following this very short time in Paris, they went on sick furlough once again and this was probably due to the fact that Flossie Violet was born on October 14, 1898.

Margaret is in the front row holding baby Louisa, and son George Ernest is seated in front of her. George and Edwin (Ted) are seventh and eighth from the left in the last row. Canadian *War Cry*. May 30, 1896. Courtesy of The John E. T. Milsaps Collection, Houston Metropolitan Collection Research Center. Houston Public Library. Houston, Texas. With permission The Salvation Army Archives, Canada and Bermuda Territory.

RIDGETOWN, ONTARIO

On November 1, 1898, the Paytons took command of the Ridgetown Corps. There is a record of their sales of the *War Cry* plus two very short reports.

> Ridgetown.-Three days special meetings, Comrades from St. Thomas and Chatham for week-end. On Monday night oyster supper. Blenheim soldiers came over for the meeting. Ensign and Capt. Green led. Good crowds all through.—K. Watt.[153]

---

[153] Canadian *War Cry*. Mar. 18, 1899.

It is interesting to note that they were supported from the two corps that they were most related to, St. Thomas and Blenheim.

> RIDGETOWN.—Good meetings all day Sunday. Lieut. Pickle, from St. Thomas led the night meeting. Just as the meeting closed two young men came and gave themselves to God. Six souls since last report.—K. Watt. Corps Cor.[154]

As of April 10, 1899, the Paytons went on sick furlough again. There are two reports that they remained active to a certain extent. Blenheim was very close to Ridgetown, and on two occasions they were invited to visit there as these reports illustrate:

> BLENHEIM.—The latest is a Junior's Jubilee, which was well attended. A first-class program with Capt. Payton as chairman. Everybody delighted. Music by brass band, autoharp, concertina, guitar, and mouth-organ. Capt. And Mrs. Huntington are getting along well and pushing the battle to the gates. Beautiful meetings yesterday and good crowds.-Ina Groom, Corps Cor.[155]

> BLENHEIM.—What next? Oh, glorious news! Had Capt. and Mrs. Payton with us for week-end, Saturday night marched down to the Central Hotel with brass band, autoharps and accordion, where a good open-air was held for 45 minutes returning to the barracks where another lively meeting was held. Sunday, glorious day, good crowds, and best of all two souls saved. Capt. Huntingdon is a hustler for getting up special meetings. Nine since taking charge.—Ina Groom.[156]

---

[154] Canadian *War Cry.* Apr. 15, 1899.
[155] Canadian *War Cry.* May 20, 1899.
[156] Canadian *War Cry.* July 8, 1899.

Second row from left to right: Margaret, Louisa, George, first row: Flossie and Edwin.

BUFFALO No. 7, NEW YORK

February 5, 1900, George and Margaret were transferred to the United States and took charge of the Buffalo No. 7 Corps. From research in the *War Cry* on both sides of the border, this was quite common in those days. There is confirmation of their being stationed in Buffalo from the list of officers in The Salvation Army Archives at National Headquarters. There is little more than that. The *War Cry* magazine for the period tells us that George had an outstanding ministry with the sales of the magazine; the purchase increased from an average of 100 to 150. In February, sales increased again to 175 immediately and were as high as 550. A grandson states that he once saw a lengthy list of George's *War Cry* customers in the Black Rock section of the city. Unfortunately that list has been lost.

While in Buffalo, George took ill and underwent surgery at the Roswell Park Cancer Institute. The doctor advised him to leave his stressful life. This required him to resign the tension-filled Salvation Army officership and return to Canada where a radical life style change took place. That is another story which we need to share at length.

George's younger brother Edwin, whom we met earlier, had resigned his officership and had moved to Port Arthur, Ontario. According to the *War Cry*, not only did Edwin go out West, but his older brother William spent some months there also. Two references of his presence there are found in the *War Cry* issues dated July 21 and August 18, 1900. For the short time that William was in that city, he became active in the Corps, and in fact, wrote the second of the following two articles.

> PORT ARTHUR.—The past week has indeed been one we can thank God for. We have had some wonderful meetings, but Sunday was the crowning time. Gospel shot [Specific evangelist Scripture verses] was fired with telling effect by both officers and comrades. In the evening the hall was packed, and the lesson from Isaiah 53:5 "With His stripes we are healed," was dealt with. Oh, how they listened, and thank God two precious souls came and sought and found the Healer of their souls. We wound up with a praise meeting. One sister got so happy she could not keep the tears away, but thank God it was for joy. Thank God the work is reviving. Hallelujah! Wm. E. Payton, Bandsman, for Ensign Hayes.[157]

There is documentation in a September 1900 *War Cry* that George, Margaret and their three children arrived in Port Arthur, "Since our last report we have welcomed Capt. and Mrs. Dayton, [Payton] from Buffalo, with their three Juniors."[158] The next chapter of their story is an unusual one of an entirely different nature.

---

[157] Winnipeg *War Cry*. Aug. 18, 1900.
[158] Winnipeg *War Cry*. Sept. 8, 1900.

Chapter Twelve

Pioneering in Western Ontario

"Finish your outdoor work and get your fields ready; after that, build your house."

Proverbs 24:27 NIV

With instructions from the doctor to "go where it is quiet as your nerves are so bad that it is affecting your digestion and general health" (reportedly caused by stomach ulcers), George decided to accept an offer by the Canadian government to homestead in the community of Dorion, Ontario, that was just being organized. The government was offering plots of 160 acres for the price of one dollar with the condition that within one year, an 18´ x 20´ house would be built, and at least one acre or more would be cleared with a garden planted.[159] His brother Edwin (who was always called Ted) had moved to Port Arthur a couple of years previously and was working there delivering milk. This undoubtedly influenced George in the summer of 1900 to move his family to Port Arthur while the house was built in Dorion.[160]

Ted also decided to accept this offer. We have seen that their brother William from Peterborough visited Port Arthur that summer. It appears that

---

[159] The majority of the material has been gleaned from three source:. Holder, Flossie. Memoir: *A Mother Remembers*. Payton, Edwin. Recorded interview with Debbie Payton Jewel 1983. *Dorion School Reunion*. 1991.

[160] Sergy, Gladys, Letter regarding Edwin and Minnie Payton.

he was in the area to help George get established.[161] While Margaret and the three children stayed in Port Arthur, the men took the forty-mile train ride to Dorion (the only transportation or communication in the area) to build the first house. When George and Ted arrived, it was necessary for them to make a trail from the train station to the properties they had purchased. Meanwhile, that fall on October 9, Harold Bach Payton was born to Margaret and George in Port Arthur. It is known that a certain Mr. Cooper had agreed to work together with George and Ted to build their houses and that the first one would belong to George. Their work literally was cut out for them

We quote an article from a 1991 publication regarding early Dorion.

> During the early years, at the turn of the century, this Northwestern part of Ontario was called New Ontario, when it was first opened for settlement. In the advertisements prepared by the government of the day, to attract settlers into New Ontario [it] was stated, 'During the winter the climate is cold but steady with a fair amount of snow. This, as all Canadians know, is more healthy and agreeable than intermittent thaws.'
>
> Most of the earliest settlers arrived in Dorion via the Canadian Pacific Railroad (C. P. R.) getting off at Wolf River Siding, the beginning of the Bishop's Trail. They assisted each other with the building of the 'shanty' homes to be ready when their wives and children arrived from Port Arthur. Many wives and children lived some months in the old Immigrant Shed, located where later the Woodside's Iron Foundry was built.
>
> The early homes were built of logs, in many instances hand-hewn with dove-tail corners. Barns too, were built from the logs cut to make room for the sowing of crops and seeding of gardens.
>
> The women hooked rugs to beautify the bare wood floors of their homes. Quilting of bed covers wasn't the mere hobby that it is today; many early settlers would have found the winter nights pretty cold sleeping without the piles of patch work quilts to cover themselves.

---

[161] Canadian *War Cry*. July 21, 1900.

Knitting, sewing, crocheting was necessary skills for the women of that long-ago time. And strong was the competition between them at the early fall fairs.[162]

With little money available, the log cabin they built conformed to the specific measurements stipulated by the government. George moved his family to their new home five days after Christmas in 1900. Margaret used to say, "It looked like they cut a square hole in the woods and dropped down a log cabin." The only sawed lumber was in the door and there was a half window. The floors were uncomfortable to walk on because of the knots that protruded from the logs. Flossie remembered that, finally, "Father purchased an adz, (a cutting tool differing from an ax because it had an arching blade set at right angles to the handle) to adz off the knots so you would not stub your toes."[163]

How they were able to build that log cabin in the short period of time from summer until Christmas with the extremely harsh winters speaks volumes to their dedication and hard work. It is imagined that having finished the house, the men returned to Port Arthur in time to celebrate Christmas with the family prior to their move to this primitive environment. We do not know what furniture they had been able to accumulate or create for the house. What were the arrangements for cooking? Did they cook over the open fire in the fireplace or did Margaret have a cast iron wood burning stove? Undoubtedly those first winter months in their new house must have been extremely difficult. We can assume that the only water they had that winter was melted snow. The children were Louisa (six), Edwin (four), Flossie (two), and Harold who was only six weeks old. Because the branches of the trees were so close to the house, George cut down some more trees so light could get in.

The three men obtained a contract from the railroad company to take out the ties (probably removing ties and replacing them with new ones). They finished it in the spring, but did not get paid. Eventually they had no money, and at times all they had to eat was dry bread and tea. One day while George was away, he found some blueberries so he filled his lunch pail with his discovery. When he arrived home late that night, the children were all asleep. He told Margaret to "get the children up." He said, "I can't eat any of these knowing they went to bed hungry." The children were awakened and enjoyed

---

[162] *Dorion School Reunion* 1991.
[163] Holder, Flossie.

the blueberries along with their parents. By the end of the summer, the men took the contract to Port Arthur and bartered with a grocery store in return for much needed groceries.[164]

George's brother Ted had been delivering milk in Port Arthur and decided to start a dairy farm. In order to obtain his first cow, he had to return to Port Arthur and walk the cow back following the railroad tracks. It took him three days to accomplish this.

There was no church so every Sunday Margaret would put the best tablecloth on the table and everyone sat around it. Each had a Bible and a Salvation Army song book so they had their Sunday school service and established their Army teaching in their hearts and minds. It is probable that Ted, whose house was across the road, would join them in this family worship. When the children were older, George taught them how to play brass instruments. George and one of the girls played cornet, another played alto horn and Edwin played the bass part on the baritone. Harold was integrated into the band when he became old enough.[165]

Later some Baptist families moved into the community, and they built a church about four miles away by way of the road. They were grateful for a shortcut which considerably shortened their walk to church. Edwin and Harold used to tell the story about an incident that took place one Sunday morning in that Baptist Church. After taking part in the Sunday school, they were seated in the church during the morning worship service, and the children were rustling some papers they had from the previous activity. Suddenly, one of them received a "missile" on the back of his head. It was the church hymnal delivered from the hands of their father, and they knew enough not to turn around. The Paytons attended the Baptist services, but they still maintained their Salvation Army family worship each week. Harold's family still has a book in which his name was inscribed that was given to him by the Baptist Sunday School. In the census report of 1911, the Payton family plus one other were listed as Salvationists in spite of the fact that the nearest corps was forty miles away.

Having been a blacksmith prior to Salvation Army officership, George was unusually adept at improvising. His children were amazed when he was able to make a water pump from wood and a piece of leather as a diaphragm.

---

[164] Holder. Flossie.
[165] Payton, Edwin. Recorded interview 1983.

When Edwin saw that his father was successful in bringing up water from the well, he was quoted as saying that his father was the "smartest guy in the world." Cousin Harold also remembers hearing Flossie say that she thought that her father was a magician when she saw the water coming from the spout.

The log cabin as it is was eventually developed. Note the wooden pump at the corner of the house.

George eventually purchased a windmill, and instead of erecting a tall pole he stripped a tree of all of its branches and attached the windmill to the top. That stood for many years as attested to by Nell and Alberta (granddaughters) when they visited years later.

In order to provide some entertainment for the children, Margaret read two or three chapters each night from one of the literary classics. From this practice, they remembered such books as *Treasure Island, Samantha at Saratoga, Mr. Midshipman Easy,* and *Around the World in 80 Days.* One Christmas George and Margaret promised the children that Santa Claus was going to visit them, and they were convinced that he was a real person. They wondered how he would arrive and if he would have to climb down one of the nearby trees. What they received on Christmas morning looked wonderful to them. Actually they were only some used toys that had been repaired and painted. They didn't recognize that they were refurbished.

Left to right—Flossie, Edwin, Margaret, Harold, George, Louisa and Jack, the dog.

As there was little to entertain the children, they remembered details that to others might seem insignificant. Flossie recalled a red rooster they named Peter that took it upon himself to protect the hens. The problem was the chicken hawks would perch in the trees and try to snatch them. When Peter saw a hawk, he would chase the hens into hiding, run to the kitchen door and make a loud noise. When Margaret heard him, she would go outside. When she was with Peter, he would stop making the noise and walk beside her. When she would go in the house, he knew all was clear so he made a call, and the hens would come out into the open again.

Another source of entertainment for the children was their dog Jack. He was part wolf, but he was a great pet and would join them when they played hide and seek. He would go and hide, and when they would go looking, they would see his nose peeking around a corner. Jack was also a sleigh dog. Their father made a harness for him, and in winter, Jack would pull them around on the sleigh. That was fine until a rabbit came into view—then he would take off.

As boys will do, Edwin and Harold played war games, but they lacked equipment with which to pretend. One day they came across a couple of steel rods. George's shop was well equipped so they took advantage of the emery wheel and sharpened the ends to make spears. While one pumped the wheel, the other did the sharpening. Upon completion of the task, they inadvertently left a groove in the middle of the wheel. Their father, George, was not happy with them and gave them the task of leveling off the wheel again using a grinding stone. After a very lengthy effort, they were able to eliminate the groove.

Life was rugged. It consisted of constant hard labor in order to survive. The immediate job was to clear more land which was a slow process. First, the virgin timber was cut down and the stumps removed. Son Edwin used to explain that sometimes they set a fire in the stumps; however, mostly it was a matter of hacking away at the roots until a team of horses could pull it out. Some people just pulled the stumps onto their sides and created "stump fences."

The first summer they were in Dorion, George met a man who had a log house on some cleared land approximately five miles away. He decided to leave so he said that George and his family could use the house and plant a garden since they still didn't have enough land cleared for their needs. When they arrived, they started a fire in the fireplace to warm the house, but soon they felt the stings of bees. The man had chinked moss between the logs, and the bees made their nests there. It was no small task to get rid of them.

One day they decided to return to their own house, and while walking they could see a fire in the distance. As they approached their house, it was clear that the place was in danger of catching fire. Margaret took baby Harold, and another man took Flossie, and they ran to a safe distance. George remained and kept pouring water on the house in an effort to save it. In the end, everything was black from the smoke, but it was not lost.

Any groceries or other commodities had to be ordered from Port Arthur some forty miles away. Since the train did not stop in Dorion, the conductor threw whatever was to be delivered off the train as it ran through their property. There was no telling what condition the merchandise would be in after such a rough delivery. For instance a one-hundred pound bag of sugar ended up in a puddle.

One time a couple of railroad workers who had been hunting in the area asked to stay for the night. George told them that the only place they could sleep would be in the kitchen. They accepted this arrangement, but in the morning, they said they hadn't been able to sleep because mice were running all over them. The visitors said they would be passing through on the train, and if someone would be at the railroad track, they would throw off a cat in a bag. They followed through with their promise except the cat in a bag turned out to be a mother cat with seven kittens. That night nobody slept very much because the cats made so much noise catching the mice.

When it came to treating illnesses, the doctor was too far away to contact, so Margaret referred to a book written by Doctor A. W. Chase. The book provided her with advice and remedies in addition to some old family therapies and cures that had been handed down over the generations. If one of them had a serious illness, it was necessary to travel to Port Arthur to see a doctor.

Within a year or two, the government started to build roads, and George held the position of road superintendent for many years. The money he earned from this employment helped him to pay men to clear the family property.

Second row—Edwin (Ted), first row—Edwin, Margaret, Jack (the dog), Harold, George, Louisa, Flossie, Grandfather Edward Payton.

There was no school so Margaret was the children's teacher for five years. In 1905, a one-room school house was built about a mile from their house. On the first day of school, the carpenter was still planing one of the benches, and the shavings were all over the floor. This turned out to be Edwin's bench. There were twelve students when they started, and four of them were Paytons. That first year they only held school from July to Christmas.

There were two community activities which were highlighted each year. One was the Sunday School Picnic. Everyone in the township went to it and enjoyed the get-together. The second activity was the Christmas program organized by the church for the children. There was a Christmas tree and a Santa Claus with gifts for everyone. All the children had to memorize something for the program. Flossie remembered one rhyme that she had to quote:

> What would you give for me Papa
> If somebody wanted to buy
> And offered you bright shinny dollars
> And piled them as high as the sky?
>
> They say you are good at a bargain
> So tell me as true as can be
> If I was put on the market
> What would you give for me?

"The 1991 Dorion School Reunion" corroborates references to the two special annual events, and we quote what was said about one of them:

THE FIRST OF JULY PICNIC

There were two annual events held during the early years of Dorion that no one would voluntarily miss, the School Christmas Concert and the First of July Picnic.

The picnics were held on the grounds of the Farmers' Club Hall. Sports events provided the main activity during the day with a "whooping" dance held in the hall that night. The dance ended only when the musicians, local people, were just plain too tired to play for even one more square.

The chance to visit with neighbors living miles away was one of the women's favorite picnic pleasures. Food was featured, for after all, what is a picnic without stacks of tasty food? The women outdid themselves preparing their choicest cakes, pies, pickles, salads and meats. There was a great deal of rivalry about it, too.

The men folk gossiped too, about crops, cost of farm goods, and the weather. To early settlers on the land, the weather was of prime importance, even though nothing could be done about its vagaries. The weather could make the difference between a good comfortable winter, or a trying one . . . good or bad crops!

Races, ball games, horse shoe pitching and tugs-of-war gave young and old alike the chance to show their prowess. Everyone came, from babes-in-arms to the most aged grandpas and grandmas.

Surprisingly enough, . . . our pioneer settlers dressed in their best for the picnic. White shirts and ties were in order for the men, full flowing, best dresses and their best flowered or feathered hats anchored on with dagger-like hatpins were the ladies' choice of picnic attire.[166]

With the advent of the windmill, the settlers had the benefit of power for pumping water and grinding grain. The grain hopper was level with the barn floor. One Sunday morning, Flossie was all decked out in a new print dress. She decided to go to the barn where Edwin and Harold were standing on one side of the hopper watching the grain go down. She decided to go on the other side of the hopper where the shaft was turning. It was a very windy day, and her dress caught in the shaft and pulled her tight to the machine. Flossie called for her father who was in the stable below. He tried to get her untangled, but the strong wind was turning the millwheel fast which caused the shaft to rotate at a high rate. Flossie's father and two brothers tried to turn the millwheel out of the wind but they were not successful. Her dress was pulled so tight that her skin was bruised. Her father had a pen knife with which he cut the dress off, freeing her from the rotating shaft. He then ran, carrying her to the house and put her on a table to check her over. She was put to bed for a week to make sure that she was going to be all right. While in bed, Flossie made doll dresses from what remained of her new dress.

---

[166] Dorion School Reunion 1991.

As the children grew older, two things happened. They were given chores on the farm. They also organized a group of ten they called "The Cheerful Wigglers." They would go to each other's homes to play games, sing songs together and have a lunch. Sometimes the home visits were a surprise to the owner. In any case, they had fun times. Occasionally they would put on programs at the club house (built in 1912) in order to raise funds for their activities. On one occasion they used a large zinc tub with which to take up the collection. It would have been obvious if someone did not contribute since coins were the order of the day and would have clinked as they dropped into the tub. In the winter they had horse drawn sleigh rides.

Regarding the chores, Louisa helped her mother in the house and Edwin, Harold and Flossie worked outside. On the farm, Edwin was given the job of driving the horses while plowing or planting potatoes. Chores such as feeding animals and milking cows had to be covered as well, so the four of them had plenty to do. Years later, while in their Ithaca summer home, when Edwin saw a farmer plowing his field he would say, "To the bush, to the road." His children had no idea what he was talking about until they saw a simple drawing of the property in Dorion. These two commands were clearly explained as the drawing depicted the road in the front of the house and a distance behind it, the bush (trees) could be seen. They obviously did their field work on the farm following that pattern.

In the winter, George and his sons occupied themselves cutting ice from the river with which to store the milk in the warmer weather. They couldn't cut ice from the bay because it would freeze solid to the bottom so they had to go where river water was running below. The ice would be as much as four feet thick. George would cut the ice, and when it was brought up to the ground, they broke it into blocks. The blocks were then taken to the ice house where it was packed in sawdust to keep it from thawing during the summer months. They never ran out of ice. They also cut down trees and trimmed the logs in addition to accumulating pulp wood to be sold in Port Arthur.

One cold winter day, George and Edwin went to the general store which was also the post office. While Edwin waited outside, George went in and was told that the temperature was 64 degrees below. He returned to the sleigh and said, "Turn around the horses and let's go home. This is too cold for man or beast." Edwin commented, "What about me?"

Walking in the snow was not an easy task either. Edwin talked about walking to school on snow shoes. One time George, Harold and Edwin were walking in the snow together. Harold was endeavoring to equal the long strides of his father's footsteps by trying to place his feet in the imprints in the snow. He even tumbled a few times. At one point, he turned around and said to Edwin, "I don't know where I am going, but when I get there I'll be glad for I am following in the footsteps of my dear old dad." Edwin used to share the fact that sometimes they had snow ball fights in July. This was due to the fact that the sunshine could not reach some of the snow piled up in the valleys, and it would not melt until well into the month of July.

In addition to being the Road Superintendent, George became a Justice of the Peace in the District of Thunder Bay. His greatest endeavors, in addition to the farm, were the establishment of a blacksmith shop and a sawmill.

Early establishment of the sawmill.

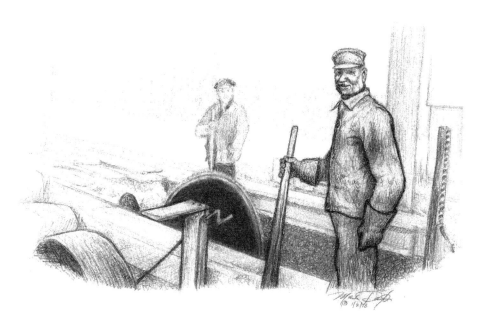

George at the sawmill after the fire.
Artist—Mark Payton

Flossie at age fourteen.

Harold on top of the hay wagon.

Note the windmill in the background.

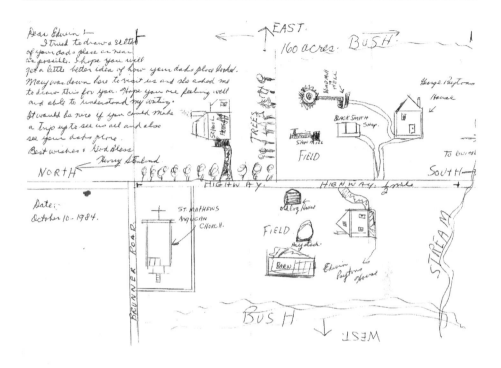

Hand drawing of the area around the Payton farms as drawn
by Henry Stenlend at Edwin Payton's request.

    The profits from the sawmill were a boon to their income, and the business occupied much of their time. Edwin's first job in the sawmill was to fire the boiler, but that was only until Harold was old enough to handle that task: Edwin was then responsible to carry away the lumber that George cut. Flossie was just as much involved in this heavy work. All went well with the sawmill until one night Margaret awoke and everything outside was unusually bright. The mill was on fire! They didn't have the equipment to put it out, but some neighbors came to assist. With their help, by means of a bucket brigade, they emptied two water wells but were not able to save the mill. They had prepared a car-load of lumber that was prepared to ship. The box car was on the siding ready to be loaded the next day, but the fire consumed it all. It was eventually determined that the fire was caused by arson. George was an excellent mechanic and within a few months he had the sawmill running again.

Early stages of the second house (1913).

With the advent of the sawmill George was able to build a second house with the help of the children. This was built with sawed lumber so it had adequate doors and windows. It had a second floor, and eventually they covered the house with black tar paper. One can imagine that it contained more modern equipment of the time making Margaret's life a little easier.

Another day to remember is what they called "The Bush Fire." The children were not able to go to school as the fire was burning just across the road. Again, they did not have adequate equipment to fight the fire. All they could do was take pails of water to put out small fires caused by the burning bark flying off the trees. The fire came so close that they thought the house would be destroyed. George dug a large hole outside the dining room window. Margaret gathered their clothes and other important things and put them on the table, ready to remove if the fire got dangerously close to the house. The plan was that she would pass them through the window, and George would put them in the hole and cover them. Fortunately, that was not necessary. At three in the afternoon, it went black as night with smoke and soot. When it was over, they were all black but had been able to save everything.

In 1912 George once again became ill with similar symptoms to those he had suffered back in Buffalo, New York, in the spring and summer of 1900.

He went to Port Arthur for treatment, but prior to going, he asked the Lord to give him four more years in order to see all of his children reach some maturity. He was operated on for cancer and was able to return to the farm and sawmill in Dorion. He was in fairly good health for about three more years.

News of the tragic maritime accident which caused the loss of the ship "Empress of Ireland" on May 29, 1914, and the loss of many Salvationists traveling to London, England, for the International Congress quickly reached the small community of Dorion through the telegraph office at the railroad station. Margaret promptly went to the station to obtain any information she could. She sat there in tears as the names of the lost (many of whom were her friends) gradually came over the teletype.

In 1915 the Ontario Province established a potato-growing contest for the purpose of introducing new potato hybrids. Each participant had to grow certain types of potatoes. George decided that Edwin was going to win the challenge. The contestants had to be young, and each a farmer's son. They picked out a certain field, and after planting the potatoes, they sprinkled ashes from the sawmill furnace on the rows to enhance the growth. Edwin was the winner for the province in the trial for crop yield. The prize consisted of a trip to Guelph, Ontario, where he participated in a course in livestock and seed judging. Travel expenses for the round trip to Guelph were supplied.

While away from the family, George wanted Edwin to visit his brother William in Peterborough. While there he came in touch with a vibrant Salvation Army corps, and he dated his spiritual birth from that visit. Also while there, he became acquainted with his cousin Herbert, who had already signed up for military service as the First World War was in progress. Edwin wrote and asked permission from his parents to join the service to which they reluctantly agreed. The story of Edwin's service in England and his participation in the famous battle of the Somme in France is a story to be told at another time. This meant that back on the farm, there was one less hand to cover the chores. Flossie and Harold stepped into the breach and helped their father with the sawmill and other chores.

In 1916 George became ill. When he went to the doctor, he was told that the cancer had returned, but there was no further medical help available to him. Doctor Bryan said "Mr. Payton, in 1912 you asked God for four years." The visit to the doctor was in October 1916, and he died on January 20, 1917. In the fall before George died, he was able to harvest ten acres of potatoes by driving the horses pulling the potato digger. They got the potatoes into pits, and Harold (sixteen) and Flossie (eighteen) bagged them in one-hundred pound bags and stored them in the root house. They were not able to get any help because all the young men were off to war. After that, they were able to get wood from the bush for the oncoming winter. Flossie and Harold each took a horse and fastened a log to it which was then brought up to the house until they had enough wood. One of their neighbors had a power saw and cut it up for them.

When George died, the corps officer along with Sergeant Major Henderson traveled to Dorion to conduct the funeral. The Sergeant Major and his wife had become close friends of the family. George was a member of the Home Guard during the war which took him to Port Arthur to guard the grain elevators. Whenever he was in Port Arthur, he was faithful to The Salvation Army there. During these visits, his friendship with the Hendersons flourished. At the time of his father's death Edwin was in a hospital in England recovering from a minor injury. An orderly walked through the large ward and dropped mail on the patients' beds. At first he didn't pay much attention to the single card he received. It was from his sister Flossie which told him of their father's death. Edwin used to refer to that day as the saddest one in his life.

On November 11, 1918, when Edwin was working in the telephone and telegraph office in the Bramshott Camp in the south of England, he received early word of the impending signing of the Armistice that ended the First World War. Because there were so many Canadian troops stationed in Europe, it was impossible to return all of them to their home country right away. For those awaiting repatriation, the Canadian government established The Khaki University where the soldiers could study. Since Edwin had been able to spend only four years in that one-room school house, he elected to take advantage of this opportunity.

When it came time for him to return home, he notified his mother, and she arranged to travel to Peterborough to meet him. They spent some time with George's brother William and family. From there they traveled to Rochester, New York, to visit with Margaret's brother Richard William, the one who introduced the Bach family to The Salvation Army. Although he and his wife were no longer officers, they remained active Salvationists in that city for many years.

Quite some time had passed since Edwin had been discharged from the military, but when it came time to travel back to Dorion, his mother asked that he wear his uniform. It was a good thing that he did because when they were on the train traveling west, they learned that the train was not scheduled to stop in Dorion which meant that they would have to pass by Port Arthur and then return on another train. Margaret, as Edwin stated, "did a sob story on the conductor," and noting the uniform, the gentleman assured them that he would have the train stop in Dorion. When they arrived, there was a crowd at the train station to meet them. Edwin stated, "Boy, that was one of the biggest moments in my life, the war was over and I was home."

Edwin Payton in Canadian military uniform.

But what were they to do when it came to the farm. Harold was on his own, and Edwin had seen the world and wasn't about to go back to the hard life of farming on land carved out of the bush. Louisa and her husband, Gilbert Bryant, and Flossie and her husband, Albert Holder, had moved to

Port Arthur. It was decided that the two brothers would sell the farm and move to Port Arthur as well. With the money from the sale of the property, Edwin and Harold bought a house and settled there.

The fact that the Payton family left its mark on that small community was proven when, in 1956, Edwin with his wife and family were visiting there for Edwin's last time. They stopped at a gas station, and one of his sons asked an attendant if he had any memory of the Payton name in Dorion. After some thought, the attendant asked if he was referring to The Salvation Army people.

Left to right surrounding Uncle Ted—Edwin, George, Ernest, Frank, Elsie Payton and Ted's grandson.

Edwin's first employment was painting ships, but he wasn't happy doing this. Through the assistance of someone in the city government, he was able to take advantage of his signal corps experience during the war and found employment in the telephone office. We do not know what work Harold was able to obtain but think that it might have been in carpentry as he later listed this as his profession when he applied to be a Salvation Army officer. This probably was true with Gilbert Bryant, the husband of Louisa. The Bryants had two children, George born on October 22, 1917, and Max born on September 20, 1920.

Third row, second from the left, Gilbert Bryant, third Edwin Payton and sixth, Harold Payton. Second row, seventh from the left, Louisa Bryant. First row, from the left, first and second are Sergeant Major and Mrs Henderson and sixth is Margaret Payton.

Little is known of the family's time in Port Arthur. It is possible to piece together a few things that have been heard from family members plus some reports from the Canadian *War Cry*.

They immediately became active in the Port Arthur Corps for there is a report of Edwin and Harold's enrollment as soldiers in the *War Cry* issue dated February 21, 1920. This would have been only a matter of weeks after Edwin first returned to Dorion. Proof of their activities in the corps is in the report in the issue dated June 26, 1920, where it was stated: "The Captain has organized a band and the bandsmen are practicing hard with their instruments, and soon the streets of Port Arthur will resound with Salvation music." Since it is known that the Paytons used to play their horns in their morning Sunday School, it is logical that they were the musicians who started a band shortly after their arrival.

Today, there is one city at the head of Lake Superior, Thunder Bay, but for many years there were two—Port Arthur and Fort William. At the same time, there were two corps, and they often joined together for special events. There is a report of the Port Arthur Corps comrades joining with the Fort William people during a series of revival meetings. On one occasion, the Fort William band joined in the dedication of a men's hostel in Port Arthur.[167] However, since there was a spirit of competition between the two cities, this also held true when it came to the two corps. We have heard stories to this effect from Edwin and Harold. Proof of this is also found in the *War Cry* when the two corps were competing to see which one could sell the most *War Cry* magazines.[168]

During the short period of time that the Payton family lived in Port Arthur, there were frequent changes of officers. In spite of this, the corps reported good progress and there were several special activities to interest the people. There was a time when a special guest visited the corps—a missionary from India. To encourage curiosity on the part of the public, the visitor dressed six of the children in Indian costumes, and they paraded through the streets along with the soldiers and the band. Perhaps the most outstanding event during their time in Port Arthur was the visit of the Winnipeg Corps Band. This raised enough interest on the part of the public that the local newspaper, *The Port Arthur News-Chronicle* noted the following:

> The Salvation Army Band of Winnipeg played its way into the hearts of Port Arthur citizens last evening at the Musical Festival given in the St. Paul's Presbyterian Church. Their instruments are superb examples of the silversmith's art. For clarity of tone the music has never been excelled, not even by the famous British Bands that have visited the head of the lakes. There is not a reed instrument amongst them. It is a genuine wind band. The absence of reeds was noticeable in such a number as "Soul Pictures" which concluded with an excerpt from Tannhause, but the other numbers

---

[167] Winnipeg *War Cry*, April 26, 1919.
[168] Winnipeg *War Cry*. June 3, 1922.

were so arranged that the music uttered by the wind instruments was sufficient for the purpose.[169]

The last special event in which the Payton family participated while in Port Arthur was the annual Harvest Festival activities including the auction to raise money for their contribution to Headquarters. They may have remained there except for a terrible tragedy which might have been the catalyst for their moving again.

It was the last day before the 1920 Christmas vacation when Albert Holder (husband of Flossie) was working on the construction of a grain elevator. He was on a belt at the top of the building when another worker decided to test the belt system. The worker did not give a warning and threw the switch. Albert was thrown headlong to the ground level and died instantly. Flossie's first child, Nell, had been born on November 17, 1918, and her second daughter, Alberta, was born after the accident on May 23, 1921. According to Flossie, this horrible accident severely affected her. The family may have felt that it would be better that they move away from the area.

According to Edwin, he and Harold traveled by ship to Hamilton. Perhaps this was because they were single and were sent on ahead to find a place where the families could live. On October 30, 1922, the rest of the family started a new life in Hamilton, Ontario. It is probable they decided to live in Hamilton where Cousin Herbert Payton was the corps officer of the Hamilton No. 2 Corps. At first all of the families lived together in one house. After Gilbert and Louisa Bryant found their own place, Margaret, Edwin, Harold, Flossie and her two daughters shared one house.

---

[169] Winnipeg *War Cry*. July 22, 1922.

Chapter Thirteen

Who Was George Charles Payton?

Under a spreading chestnut tree
The village smithy stands;
The smith a mighty man is he,
With large and sinewy hands;
And the muscles of his brawny arms
Are strong as iron bands.

Henry Wadsworth Longfellow
The Village Blacksmith

George Charles Payton.

Most families have fond memories of their Grandpa such as sitting on his lap listening to stories of family history, reading a children's story book, playing on the floor with him or helping him in the garden. This was not the case with George Charles Payton. His death in 1917, at the age of 49, preceded the birth of all twenty of his grandchildren. His youngest son, Harold, was sixteen, and his eldest daughter, Louisa, was twenty-two. Family lore, some oral history and a few pictures is the sum of the knowledge that his grandchildren have of him. Living a pioneer life meant there was little to leave to his children. Of his possessions, we can list his hunting rifle, part of his anvil, a spike he created and one of his Justice of the Peace books.

He was a skilled and talented man. In his early years he apprenticed and became a blacksmith, and in his early twenties he met The Salvation Army and became a musician and later a captain. When he homesteaded 160 acres north of Lake Superior, he became a pioneer, hunter, farmer, sawmill operator, road supervisor, and later, the Justice of the Peace

This does not tell us much about the man. What were his inner thoughts and beliefs or his outlook on life? One of the possessions not mentioned above was his Bible. His daughter Flossie was the keeper of this special piece of history. At the wedding of his grandson George, his Aunt Flossie presented to him his grandfather's Bible. It bore his grandfather's name and rank as a Salvation Army officer, the same as his. It was old and tattered with many loose pages. This sacred book would reveal much about the man George Charles Payton.

The inscription on the front of the Bible reads:

"Captain Geo. C. Payton
From Rev. J. Rawson
Kingsville,[Ontario]"

Nothing is known about the person who gave this gift except that Kingsville, Ontario, was close to their early appointments. George profusely underlined passages throughout the Bible. In many places his comments are on the top, the bottom and on both sides of the pages. The writing was extremely small. On many pages he would pen three lines on the bottom margin. In spite of the fact that he had a limited education and a trade (blacksmith) that did not require a large amount of reading, he had an expanded vocabulary. Words like *instinct, incomprehensible,* and *superlative* were used in his writings. On the last page of the Old Testament, he penned:

"Commenced reading Genesis March 6, finished July 22 at Malachi 4" (the Old Testament). What a formidable accomplishment in four months and sixteen days!

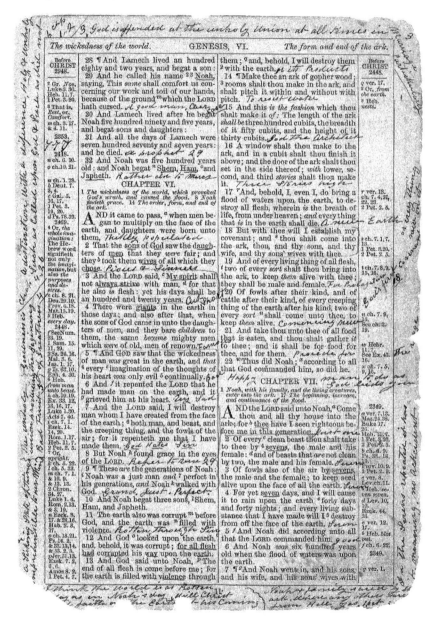

A page from George's Bible.

One puzzle that has not been solved to everyone's satisfaction is the appearance of the year 1896 twenty-nine times or more. There are three thoughts on this, (1) does it relate to the birth of their son, Edwin, (2) were there any thoughts that 1896 might be the end of time or (3) was it the year he read the Bible in late 1895 or early 1896? It appears that he read the Old Testament during the first year of officership at Essex, Ontario. Most of the Bible comments fall into three themes:

Church and Theology

The blessing of sanctification seemed to be his passion. He noted the word first appeared in Genesis 2:3. The words *sanctify* and *sanctification* were circled every time. These were the only words that received that kind of attention, and they were repeated hundreds of times.

It appears that George thought that *idolatry* was the sin of his day. On a page in Deuteronomy 12 he wrote, "Idolatry prevails everywhere this day in 1896." In Exodus 13 he quipped, "How easy to lead people into Idolatry . . . ;" and in Judges 14, he inscribed, "England and America [are] no better and continue to serve idols." These feelings were expressed throughout the Old Testament.

In many passages *The Coming of the Messiah* was noted. He clearly saw Jesus in verses in the Old Testament. The coming of Jesus and end times was recorded in the margin of many chapters.

The strict observance of the Sabbath, was an important part of George's life. Nehemiah's keeping of that holy day impressed him. On the edge of the page, he expressed his thoughts by writing, "Sabbath breaking is one of the most stupid sins committed. If there is a governor today regarding the Sabbath as Nehemiah, where is he in 1896?"

Upon reading II Kings 23 regarding the cleansing of the temple, he thought mostly of the *secular drift of the church of his day* and expressed this thought, "Such a cleansing, we need it today."

Social Behavior

Very evident were his views on social behavior. There was no doubt that they were strict and represented the nineteenth century. He passed many of them on to the twentieth century through his children.

Deuteronomy 22:5 was boxed in rather than underlined, which he seldom did. "The woman shall not wear that which pertaineth unto a man; neither shall a man put on a woman's wear." At the top margin, he wrote "Women's wear." On other pages, he deplored inappropriate and immodest dress.

Attention was brought to the saying, "spare the rod and spoil the child," a maxim that survived another generation. When the Bible cautioned signing another's loan, George added, "Don't sign a joint note."

It wasn't necessary to read between the lines to know that George was very disappointed with the *leadership of his day*. He often noted the need for principled leadership. Following are some examples.

Hezekiah: "set aside for spirituality and cleaning."

Nehemiah: "Why don't servants of this type be appointed now?" He answered his own question, "A lack of material!"

"Glory to God for such a man!"

Queen Esther: "Prayer and Fasting prevails. God always delivers on time."

Many other heroes of the Old Testament drew comment from George including: Moses, Samson, Gideon, Samuel, David and Josiah, naming a few.

It is not surprising that George saw things through the eyes of a blacksmith. When he read Micah 4:3, "They shall beat their swords into plowshares and their spears into pruning hooks," he wrote in the margin, "a big job for a blacksmith."

From oral history we knew that George was the skilled and talented man alluded to at the beginning of this chapter. From gleaning his Bible, we know that he was a very principled man with very strong values, giving a clear picture of the grandfather we never met. The depth of who he was spiritually is seen in the following *War Cry* report.

> Brother Payton, Port Arthur
> Brother George passed to his reward on Saturday, January 20th, after a serious illness from which he suffered considerably for years—cancer of the stomach. Brother Payton is among the oldest

Salvationists of the Dominion. He was enrolled as a Soldier about twenty-seven years ago and, previous to his going to Dorion (sixteen years ago), was an officer in several Ontario towns and in the States; but, on account of ill-health, had to resign. He was a loyal Salvationist to the end, and whenever he came to town was glad to take his stand and do all in his power to help The Army. He was thought a great deal of in the district where he resided.

Because of ill-health and age, he was not able to go overseas, but he did his bit as long as possible on the home guard last winter, guarding the elevators, etc. Before the end came he gathered his family around him and bade them all good-by; imploring them to follow Jesus, saying, "There is nothing like Jesus!" His last words were, "Jesus, Jesus."

While the day was cold and the place was isolated, yet over forty gathered for the funeral service, which was conducted by Ensign Oake and Young People's Sergeant Major Henderson of Port Arthur.

He has left a widow, two daughters, and two sons, who are all Salvationists. One son is in France.[170]

---

[170] Canadian *War Cry*. Mar. 17, 1917.

George Charles Payton in Home Guard Uniform.

Chapter Fourteen

Hamilton and Beyond

"Your faithfulness continues through all generations; . . . ."
Psalm 119:90 NIV

The first time that Elsie Jones met the Payton family was at the Hamilton No. 2 Corps at the Sunday New Year´s Eve service in 1922. This was her first visit to the corps, and she was somewhat shy as she entered the building. Captain Ivy Payton greeted her and asked her if she was Elsie Jones as they had received notice of her soldiership transfer from England. She soon felt at home after receiving this warm greeting from Captain Herbert Payton's wife. She noticed a family consisting of an elderly lady, two gentlemen and a mother with two children. All the adults were in uniform. One of the men (Harold) was carrying a child. She incorrectly supposed that he was the father and that Flossie was the mother. After the ladies and the children were seated, the two men took their places in the band. The Paytons had been there only a matter of months but were active Salvationists. (The Bryant family was probably in attendance as well but we don't have a record to substantiate this.)

The Hamilton II Corps Band. Captain & Mrs. Herbert Payton, the corps officers, seventh and eighth from the left in the front row, and Edwin and Harold are sixth and eighth from the left standing in the last row. With permission The Salvation Army Achives, Canada and Bermuda Territory.

The families all lived in one house until they were able to find employment and make their own living arrangements. Edwin, while in Port Arthur, had started making application to attend The Salvation Army Training College, and he continued this procedure in his new corps. As suggested in records, we assume that Gilbert Bryant and Harold Payton found employment as carpenters. Flossie Holder received a pension of sixty dollars a month due to the untimely death of her husband, but it was not sufficient to support her family. She eventually found employment and initiated the purchase of a house where she, her mother Margaret, as well as Edwin and Harold lived. Margaret cared for the children which enabled Flossie to work outside the home. After a time they transferred their soldiership to the Hamilton No. 4 Corps (Argyle) where Flossie became a local officer (lay leader). She was publically recognized in 1973 for her forty-four years of active local officership service. She held six different positions while working with both youth and adults. One of her daughters was an officer for several years, however, both of them eventually married and still live in Hamilton.

In September 1923, Edwin entered the Training College to prepare for officership. He was commissioned on June 30, 1924, and sent to his first appointment as the assistant officer in the Gravenhurst, Ontario, Corps. (This was one of his mother's previous appointments.)

On November 1, 1923, Harold married Esther Evans. Esther and Elsie Jones, previously mentioned, were friends in Manchester, England, prior to their move to Canada. They would eventually marry brothers.

In 1924/5 Gilbert and Louisa Bryant moved to Rochester, New York, undoubtedly because Richard William Bach, Louisa's uncle, was living there and would help them get settled and find employment. While there, Hilda, Gilbert and Harold were born. Gilbert, the father, worked as a carpenter. In July of 1927, Gilbert and Louisa were accepted as Salvation Army officers in a special in-service training program. They held appointments in the Western New York Division for approximately twelve years, at which time they resigned and moved to Ithaca, New York. They became active Salvationists holding local officer positions. Later they moved to Detroit, Michigan, continuing their activities in the Army.

Following Gilbert and Louisa's example, Harold and Esther moved to Rochester in 1926/27 where Harold found employment as a carpenter. Their daughters Lillian and Esther, were born there. In April 1928 Harold and Esther entered the same in-service training program as the Bryants did. While in their several appointments in New York State, Ivy, Harold, Edwin, George and Marion were born. They served in six corps until 1950 when Harold became a victim to the same disease as his father and was Promoted to Glory at the same age. Esther continued as an active officer for another year until, due to illness, she was forced to retire and accept a pension.

Edwin married Elsie Jones on September 21, 1927, and singly and together, they served in eleven corps in Canada. In 1930 they were transferred to the United States where they served in thirteen corps appointments until their retirement in 1961. While stationed in Campbellton, New Brunswick, their son Ernest was born. After being transferred to the United States, George, Frank and Margaret were born.

In spite of the fact that George and Margaret's family had been forcefully separated from the influence of The Salvation Army ministry for seventeen years in western Ontario, they all eventually made this organization their place of worship, service and ministry.

This leaves us with Margaret. She remained a faithful soldier in the Hamilton No. 4 Corps (Argyle) and later in the Hamilton No. 6 Corps. Besides caring for her two grandchildren, Nell and Alberta Holder, she was active in children's ministry. This is demonstrated in a photograph of her with children from their corps in an activity they called, "The Band of Love." She was Promoted to Glory on January 20, 1945, exactly 28 years to the day after her husband George's death.

The legacy that Margaret and George left behind continues to this day. As has been documented, all of her children remained active Salvationists for the rest of their lives. Five of her grandchildren, became Salvation Army officers, one serving in overseas appointments. Many others of that generation remain active in the Army or have chosen other churches. There are those who may not have become active in a church, but their lives have demonstrated the ethics they learned from their Army upbringing. In the next generation, five became officers, and some of them also served in overseas appointments.

George's older brother William and his wife Sara Clark remained active soldiers of the Peterborough, Ontario, Corps. Eventually William relinquished the leadership of the band but always remained an enthusiastic musician. His grandchildren remember him teaching beginners in the kitchen of their home. They had six children, two of whom died as infants. The other four were faithful Salvationists. Ethel May studied music in the Toronto Conservatory of Music and wrote several vocal compositions. She was the assistant songster leader and leader of the singing company (children's choir) for many years. Violet Pearl became an officer, eventually studying to be a nurse. Later she became the administrator of several different Salvation Army hospitals in Canada. In her last appointment she was the Women's Social Services Secretary supervising all of the Salvation Army hospitals in Canada. The youngest sister, Beulah Maud, had an outstanding voice and, for several years was a soloist with the Peterborough Songsters until she married Harry Grier. After their marriage they moved away from Peterborough. William's son, Herbert, became an officer and served in six corps in Canada. He and his wife later transferred to the United States and served in thirteen corps in the USA Central Territory. They had nine children, three of whom became Salvation Army officers, and all but one became active Salvationists. The youngest was a pastor who worked in prison ministry. Two of their officer children served in overseas appointments. Of the next generation, three became Salvation Army officers.

Edwin, the youngest of the four Payton sons of Edward and Mary, served for about three years as a Salvation Army officer. He was the first to move to western Ontario where he worked delivering milk in Port Arthur. He, along with George, moved to Dorion in 1900 where he established and maintained a dairy farm until he retired in 1946. He married Minnie Fryers in 1907, and they had one daughter, Mary. He and his family were active in the Anglican Church having donated the land on which the church was built. He lived the remainder of his life in Dorion until his death in 1959. In later life he was called the Santa Claus of Dorion due to his long white beard. His daughter married Joseph Edward Kay, and they had three daughters. Joseph worked in bush logging camps most of his life where Mary often served as the cook. After Joseph's death and due to declining health, Mary Kay moved to Port Arthur. Their daughters Helen, Violet and Gladys married and remained in the Port Arthur (later Thunder Bay) and Dorion areas.

We started this narration with the story of Margaret Bach's challenge before a group of atheists to which she responded with the passage, from Hebrews 9:27, part of which is the title of this book, "And as it is appointed unto men once to die . . . ." We who have had the privilege to unearth this saga leave this challenge to all readers. God has an appointment for each and every one of us. It is up to us to allow God to guide our lives and discover His plan for us. We need to embrace this with all our might knowing that God will give us the grace and power to fulfill His plan to His honor and glory.

Grandmother Payton with some of her grandchildren.

Epilogue

"So now you know the rest of the story."[171]

This statement was made by a newscaster for many years at the conclusion of his daily report. While this book is a meager attempt to tell a story, be assured that this is not everything or "the rest of the story." The entire adventure will never be told because those who created it have gone to their eternal reward. While the authors of this volume have uncovered a mountain of detail, the book constitutes a small portion of what it could have been.

Enough of what took place has been shared in this unique life experience so that it will hopefully honor God and His goodness to this clan of believers.

While the surnames of Bach, Goodchild, and Payton have appeared from time to time, the main theme of this manuscript was centered on the life of Margaret Elizabeth Phillipi Bach Payton. It is an incredible saga that would make a fabulous movie because of the unbelievable experiences that defines a life that was given totally to God and His will for her. Only the Lord could have taken that commitment and accomplished what eventually happened.

Using his computer, George researched the Payton family history as far back as 1641. In addition he accumulated considerable material which was the beginning of this project. While this proved to be most interesting, our attention was concerned with the period from about the middle of the nineteenth century. This era included the beginnings of the family history that most reflected our desire to research. We were able to obtain available

---

[171] Harvey, Paul. Paulharveyarchives.com

sources, both living and historical records. These included The Salvation Army's archives in London, Washington, Toronto and New York as well as newspapers. These offices and the local library were most helpful.

Margaret's life, our centerpiece, carries the theme of our efforts. The more we uncovered, the more incredible the story became. How one lady packed so much into one life is an astounding message. She with her husband George had five children who all became either Salvation Army officers or local officers (church lay leaders) with the exception of their child George Ernest, who died in childhood.

The remaining four siblings had twenty children while the second and third generations had many more. The point here is that this account is what happened from 1857 through the next generation. The next generation started in 1892, and they picked up the torch and carried it further. It becomes the responsibility of those of us who have followed to not only continue in the same spirit, but to make it a point to keep a record because history is being made every day as God continues to work in the lives of people.

The family will continue to expand and, at the same time, move further apart geographically. This will make it more difficult to bring the various parts together. We, the present authors, have the extraordinary privilege of living close together and, with the help of the internet, telephone and SKYPE, were able to conveniently meet weekly or as necessary.

TO THE FAMILY

In the future it will take greater efforts to maintain a complete written record. This means that when you meet at family reunions, weddings, funerals and vacations, you will need to take time to record events and interesting stories so that you can share and coordinate your individual family histories. You will have the use of additional electronic equipment to help, including the I-pad and any other new inventions that were not available to us. Start recording and writing the anecdotes and experiences that have and are currently happening because, if you don't, you will regret the loss later.

Perhaps someone should be appointed as a leader or chairman, as was done with this project, "It is Appointed unto Men." Let us also remember that we are not just recording a family tree or the history of a clan but of an adventure that God has allowed and orchestrated for His honor and glory and for us to share.

Finally, we give much credit to Frank who gave chairmanship and overall direction and hours of detailed work to bring about this labor of love. To facilitate this we are including extra pages on which to record some of your stories.

Appendix I

Sung by Margaret Bach Payton to her children

The Army A, B, Cs

Kind friend, please pay attention to what I have to say.
We're going to sing a little song, 'twas made the other day;
Just wait and we will tell you
What it is going to be,
The name of the peculiar song is The Army A, B, Cs

A is for the Army that's not afraid to die,
B is for the banner—we mean to wave it high;
C stands for Christ our Savior, He saved our souls from hell,
And *D* is for the devil, that's one you all know well.
(Repeat words of the last line only.)

E is for the enemy who tries us to upset.
F is for the fountain, into which you'll have to get.
G is for the Gospel, which we will make it straight and plain,
And *H* is for heaven, come jump into our train.

I stands for ignorant, in every town it seems,
J stands for Jesus, who died our souls to redeem;
While *K* is for the Kingdom He promised unto thee
And *L* is for the load of sin from which you might be free.

M is for mists that hang before your eyes
N is for the numbers who've had a great surprise,
While *O* just shows eternity because it has no end
And *P* is for God's promises—we mean them to extend.

Q is for the queer folks, who say there is no hell,
R is for the right folks who know their souls are well;
While *S* is for the sinners who still are going about,
And *T* is for the blessed truth we often sing and shout.

U stands for unity; we have it in our band
V stands for vanity, and that will never stand;
While *W* stands for wisdom, His gift that saves from Hell
Just come and fall down at the *X* and you'll be saved as well.

Y stands for you, and we hope that you all know
That *Z* is for the zigzag road that leads to pain and woe
From which God's grace can save you
And from sinning set you free.
So we hope that you'll find nothing wrong with the
Army A, B, Cs.

Appendix II

Interesting Facts

Margaret's father was 67 years old when she was born.

Her mother had a son when she was 51 years old.

Her father was born in the 1700s (1795). Margaret was born in 1800s (1862). Her son Harold was born in the 1900s (1900).

She was born during the early years of the Civil War and died during the last months of World War II.

She was born in Coshocton, Ohio, across the river from Roscoe, in August 1862. A great grandson (George) was born in Coshocton, Ohio, in August 1962, one hundred years later.

She lived her first years in a very small fort; in later life she pioneered in a log cabin north of Lake Superior.

She was an early convert in the Reading, England, Corps along with Edward Higgins, future General of The Salvation Army

She was appointed to Gravenhurst, Ontario, in 1890. Her son's first appointment from Training College was Gravenhurst, Ontario, in 1925.

Although she did not name either of her daughters Margaret, her name appears in the next two generations. The name George appears in the next four generations.

The last appointment for Margaret and George was in the city of Buffalo, New York, 1900. Their grandson George's last appointment was in the city of Buffalo, New York, 1995.

She served as a Salvation Army officer in three countries and on two continents.

Her children served as Salvation Army officers and lay leaders in two countries. Five of her grandchildren served as Salvation Army officers in five countries and on two continents. Five of her great grandchildren have served as Salvation Army officers in five countries and on three continents. One great grandchild has served in ministry, in The Salvation Army and other ministries, in five countries and on four continents. Other grandchildren and great grandchildren have served and are serving in The Salvation Army or in other Christian ministries as active members and as lay leaders.